A Path
to Purpose

A Path to Purpose

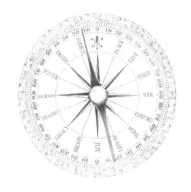

SEVEN INSPIRED STORIES
TO DISCOVER YOUR TRUE NORTH

SUSIE SCHAEFER

A Path to Purpose: Seven Inspired Stories to Discover Your True North
Published by FINISH THE BOOK PUBLISHING LLC
TEMECULA, CALIFORNIA

Some chapters contain personal recollections of a sensitive nature. In an effort to honor the personal stories of the authors, these sensitive situations have been treated with integrity while allowing the author's voice to be heard.

SCHAEFER, SUSIE, Author
A PATH TO PURPOSE
SUSIE SCHAEFER

ISBN: 978-1-7353519-3-3 (paperback)
ISBN: 978-1-7353519-4-0 (hardcover)

BIOGRAPHY & AUTOBIOGRAPHY / Personal Memoirs
BODY, MIND & SPIRIT / Inspiration & Personal Growth

Book Design by Michelle M. White
Editing by Bonnie McDermid and Amy Scott

QUANTITY PURCHASES:
Schools, companies, professional groups, clubs, and other organizations may qualify for special terms when ordering quantities of this title. For information, email Info@FinishTheBookPublishing.com.

This book is printed in the United States of America.

DEDICATION

This book is dedicated to those that have
lost their lives during the global pandemic.
You have made the ultimate sacrifice for the
global community and your lives will not be forgotten.

We also dedicate these stories to those on the front lines,
the healthcare workers and first responders who have
put the lives of others before themselves.
You embody the essence of True North by fiercely
guarding your passion and your purpose.

In addition, we must recognize the sacrifice
made by the children, who have gone without
being close to family and friends,
and whose education has been interrupted
during these challenging times.

For all those who have struggled,
may this help you regain your footing
and find your True North.

Table of Contents

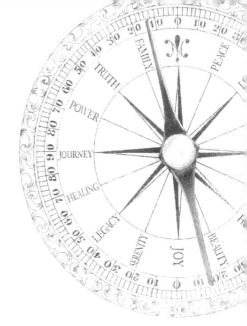

Introduction

In the fall of 2019, the thought of creating an anthology featuring multiple authors with the theme of PIVOT became not just an idea, but a calling—in part my own True North. The pull to create such a book kept coming up for me, time and again, and I knew in my heart that it would eventually come to fruition...I just didn't know how, or in what form.

Enter spring 2020 and all its changes: going from life as usual to everything we knew being upended and the rise of a global pandemic shutting down commerce and schools and creating massive shifts in our day-to-day reality. It was the beginning of a new way of life, much to our shock and surprise.

This led to the revelation I was searching for...the opportunity to create a program called **Behind the Scenes**, a six-month journey that takes aspiring authors through the process of independent publishing by writing not a whole book, but just a single chapter. Through the program, the group creates a book and learns the publishing process, working with editors and designers while the contributing authors learn in an interactive setting. The end result of the first Behind the Scenes program allows the reader of *The Pivot Project: Stories to Inspire the Shift in Your Life* to peek into the lives of people who share their own personal stories about embracing change by facing a pivot head on, not knowing the final outcome.

In our second round of **Behind the Scenes**, I asked the new group of aspiring authors if they wanted to write a second volume of *The Pivot Project*. They engaged in a wonderfully insightful conversation and landed on "Finding Your True North" as the theme for our book.

The idea behind a person's True North is similar to a compass. Whereas a compass will point towards a magnetic field, a person's True North guides them on their path and pulls them forward to find their life purpose or mission. Your True North is your inner being's voice, your calling, or what you wish to accomplish in your lifetime. A blending of your values, beliefs, and purpose, your True North is your compass for staying on track with your life.

For some, the idea of identifying their True North was a simple task, yet putting it into words was the challenge. For others, the entire idea was new and required delving deep into their soul, creating a realization they never knew existed. While every person has a true purpose on this planet, we don't always take the time to identify and embrace our calling. That is the gift in and of itself.

I find myself in awe of this group, for they have stretched themselves to go inward and write from their heart. Not only is it a sign of spiritual ascension to align with one's True North, at times it can be an uncomfortable exercise. And yet, each one wrote with passion and honesty and with the utmost transparency. When a writer pens a story from the soul, it is without doubt that it will resonate with the reader.

My hope is that the seven authors of *A Path to Purpose: Seven Inspired Stories to Discover Your True North* will inspire you to find your own True North, and to align your life's journey with the path of your best self.

These are their stories.

—Susie Schaefer, Founder
Finish the Book Publishing

Hold Your Course

Georgia Faye

The fog rolled in with no sign of leaving anytime soon. The air was cold and wet, drops of water slid down my face as I tried to see through the dense wall of water hiding my view of the world.

I was at the helm of a forty-five-foot sloop sailboat in the Saint Lawrence Seaway. When we left Montreal at noon it had been well over 90 degrees but then a sudden cold snap engulfed us. Within thirty minutes the temperature dropped below 32 degrees as the fog snuffed out the remaining light of day.

Urgent messages (in French) came over the hand-held radio to warn vessels that a nor'easter was working its way into the vicinity of the massive waterway. For the next four hours, I needed to keep watch and steer the sailing vessel through the narrow channel or we could run aground. All I had to guide me was the ship's compass, a chart plotter, and a depth-finder; the fog had swallowed up all buoy signal lights.

I'm screwed.

I was very conscious that every life on board the yacht depended upon my scant navigating skills. *I can call the crew for help,* I thought, *but they need their sleep since a big storm is heading our way. I can do this.*

Crewing the open waters of the Pacific Ocean was a far different experience because of the vast open spaces—there is a lot more room for error. If the fog rolled in, I could watch the compass heading and satellite radar (Advanced Imaging Surveillance Radar) to see where other vessels were situated, so I didn't need to worry too much about collisions or running aground. However, when you move out of your comfort zone, you're always presented with a new set of problems. If the same storm system was coming at us on the open sea, the swells would be getting steeper and I would have a lot more to deal with than a lack of bearings.

How did I get here—alone at the helm of a sailboat in a fog bank at the age of sixty-two?

We spend our entire life learning about ourselves and developing our values, beliefs, and our purpose. This journey is unique to each and every one of us. When you discover your passions and connect them to your purpose, happiness can fill your soul every day.

When we are young, we imagine ourselves doing and learning things of interest, living in certain places or living a special lifestyle, and projecting dreams we imagine can happen for us. We take those dreams, set a course for the harbors where our dreams live, and set sail.

Then the heavy weather begins—the fog rolls in, the storms come, and the winds blow us off course. We discover early that we need to grow from difficult situations. They force us to grab power from within, the grit, patience, and resilience to overcome each challenge.

When I was young, I was fortunate because I always knew I wanted to be a teacher. On any given day, you could find me down in the basement of my family's east coast Cape Cod home, teaching my stuffed bears to read and how to convert fractions to decimals or discovering a hidden country on my large world map. It was dark, dank, and cold in our cinderblock basement, but it was a world where I could imagine my dreams.

"Do you want to play a game of chess?" asked Liam from the basement stairway. My brother was desperate, as I was the only person in the house—or even on the block—that would play chess with him. Truth is, I taught him the game and eventually, he became a better and more competitive player than me.

"Only if you play student with me," I answered.

"I'm not playing that stupid game. I hate it. I'm not one of your stuffed animals to boss around."

"Come on, I'll let you read from whatever book you choose."

"Okay, I'll do thirty minutes in your classroom if you promise to play three games of chess. Winner will be the best out of three games." Liam always knew it would come down to negotiations.

I found out through our laborious chess games how to overcome challenges, analyze situations, and develop strategies to attack with back-up. This is why chess has been called the game of life—it prepares the mind for shifts, to overcome challenges, and analyze your position and alternatives. There is a beginning, a middle, and an end game with multiple shifts. Chess grandmasters study and practice for years to build a repertoire of strategies to use against formidable opponents. In life, as in chess, you can't have too many tools or strategies and you must be prepared to alter your course at any time, which is the reason I taught chess to every student in every classroom, every school, every district, and every country where I was a schoolteacher.

So, I had set a course on becoming a teacher, which meant going to four years of college. My father was a police officer and our family had money only for the essentials, so I needed to set my compass for my True North with strategies to get to my first harbor, my goal of becoming a teacher.

I had to work hard to keep my grades up during my teenage years. My father was very controlling and restricted me from most social activities except basketball, which became a passion. After years of practice, I became good enough to finish first in a foul-shooting contest in high school and then win a basketball game by throwing a wild hook shot from half court. I learned that we need an activity or sport to balance our lives and fill our souls. Later in life, my passion for sports developed into a love for sailing.

Setting your compass to your True North is the first compass point. It is the point where purpose, passion, and growing interest intersect and fuel your direction and energy. Your passion should give you joy and happiness in your everyday life. Life becomes rewarding when you realize that what's driving your interest will afford you an income to create the lifestyle you believe suits your needs.

Many of my friends didn't know their True North. Some struggled with exploring so many interests they couldn't focus. Boys who dreamed of being sport stars and girls who dreamed of being performers or actresses didn't realize they also needed a plan B if their dreams didn't come true.

My younger sister often reminds me that I was teaching school in Australia (and my father had moved on to his second wife) when she needed someone to guide her through options for a secure future. Many people remember that one person—whether it was the barber, pastor, teacher, or neighbor—who helped them discover their True North when they were lost in a fog bank. Adolescence is a difficult time indeed. At that age, we think we have all the answers and often close ourselves off to valuable input at the time we need it the most. A wise person shared with me later, "You can be young and broke or old and broke, you choose." I wish I could have shared those words with my sister at the time she needed it.

My ability to stay on course was tested later as I faced challenges I threw in my own way. I was certain that, after twelve years of private Catholic school, my values were intact, but who really knew unless one tested them? Did I truly have integrity? Was my word my word? Was I kind, generous, forgiving? Did I share with and support others when they needed me? Could I support a relationship and marriage? Could I become a good parent?

All of these questions begin to surface when you reach your twenties. When they surfaced for me, I wanted to test them out. My father always reminded me, "A woman who walks with her head high exudes confidence." It reminded me of the first solo I ever sang on our school's stage, "You'll Never Walk Alone" by Rogers and Hammerstein.

I cut my anchor to the Northern Hemisphere at the age of twenty-four and headed to the Land Down Under. I applied to fill a teacher shortage in Australia. It was another port, a safe harbor of sorts. I was armed with my greatest tool—teaching. This was to be the adventure of a lifetime. I had always dreamed of journeying to faraway places filled with romance and adventure.

I quickly went to work building my new life. I was a teacher in a fifth-grade classroom in a little school with a warm, caring staff. I built a world of colorful American expats around me. Finding adventure was the easy part; it was all around me, calling me to explore it—from the bays and harbors surrounding Sydney to the beaches, the pubs, the Outback, and the islands that were just a short airplane ride away, including New Zealand, Tasmania, Fiji, and Bali, to name a few. I was ravenous for adventure, like a tiger devouring its prey thinking it might be his last meal.

I was just as ravenous about my teaching career. It was my passion and my True North. I taught the fifth grade with a handsome co-worker who grabbed my attention the moment I walked through the door of my new school. I quickly found out he was married and unavailable. That was fortuitous, as it protected the learning environment. It also helped us become adventurous teachers who built experiences into our students' lives.

We were able to bring out the best in each other and bring it home for the students. Brad designed and built a reading loft for the classroom that looked like a castle. We gave after-school archery lessons. We designed end-of-the-year trips with overnight stays at Jenolan Caves. Each month, we took students to Sydney museums and created team scavenger hunts for afterwards. We believed experience was the best teacher and designed engaging activities to make it fun for all of us.

Life can keep us on a steady course until the fog rolls in. Three years later, Brad separated from his wife of ten years and our fleeting glances became fixed on each other. Being a romantic, I was looking for my soulmate, but Brad was looking for an opportunity to experience life outside of marriage. *Timing.*

Brad loved projects and he selected a big one for us: "Let's renovate and live in a century-old house." I must say, I was first captivated by the idea, and second, I needed the anchor he was offering me to pull away from my wild life.

After three years of living and working together, the project had taken a toll on us and we ended up in different places. I was looking for happily-ever-after and he was looking for a break; the kind where he would do his thing and I would do mine.

"I'm moving to do a year's exchange in Canada. I need an adventure and you have had plenty," said Brad.

Love is unpredictable, intangible, and often a moving target. You can see it, but you can't grab it like the ring on a merry-go-round. Timing is one of the metrics that can throw a compass into a spin, like when a magnet is set next to the magnetic compass needle. Good timing can guide you on a pathway where you can share your life with someone else and bad timing can cause it to spin out of control. I always felt luck had a lot to do with it.

Obviously, I never had much luck in that department.

I was looking for my soulmate, that special person who would understand me and give me room to grow within a relationship that provided comfort and security. I didn't want to play games or manufacture or settle for a so-called convenient relationship. I was not a hunter but responded to being hunted. I wanted my suitor to be smitten and have his words and actions come from his heart. Maybe my expectations were *too* high—I wanted the fairy tale. Over time, I realized having all the stars align happens only for the chosen few.

And then in walked Wyatt Stetson, the hunter, a headliner for the expat family. Wyatt owned a restaurant that we expats frequented. He looked like Mel Gibson and he was arrogant, cheeky, and a player. While Brad took himself off to Canada to find his adventure, Wyatt was in hot pursuit. He came with plenty of warning labels, but his timing was right. I was getting to the stage of settling down and Wyatt was looking for a woman who would make a good mother and wife. At the time I was flattered he selected me. After all, he was cited in the Sydney magazine *Sheila* as the most handsome available bachelor in the city.

His persistence paid off. One night, we fell into a passionate relationship that I couldn't control. No matter what happened or who got hurt, I couldn't steer or keep my course.

Brad returned to Sydney and, upon hearing about Wyatt, proposed marriage. Marriage with Brad was something I had dreamed of, but thought it would never happen. My compass was in a spin. Brad represented the anchor and security I thought I had been looking for, yet the freedom of uncontrollable passion brought nothing but delight.

Of course, leopards do not change their spots—a cliché, but true. I followed Wyatt to New Mexico. After we wed, he had no intention of changing his lifestyle and tried less and less to fit into the role of a father and husband as each passing year went by. It wasn't in his nature.

Our twelve rocky years together were based on passion. Wyatt's True North didn't point to being a father or a husband. I needed to protect the boys and myself, so I left silently with no alimony or support. I was grateful for the directional pull of my True North to guide me through those rough seas.

Dark times were ahead for this single sailor; I had carved out a course of rough waters for myself. *Some of us pick the easy course and some of us just make it harder for ourselves.* I focused on raising two well-grounded young men as my top priority. My attention was now on how to independently make ends meet in my world of limited time and energy.

As a primary school science teacher for twelve years, I had never thought of becoming a school administrator, but it became increasingly evident that this was the only logical way I could make ends meet, especially as the boys got older. Armed with my master's degree and an administrative credential, I took every assignment that would credit me with leadership roles. It took close to ten years to carve that change of course.

Finally, when the tide turned and a new superintendent was hired, I secured my first assignment as an assistant principal. My boys were in school, one in elementary and the other starting middle school. I made it clear I had high expectations for them while they were at school and for all behaviors while they were under my roof. (As part of the divorce, they were with Wyatt most weekends, so I had very little control over their behavior then.)

Those were the times my compass was tested daily. Each and every day I developed a mindset to do the best I could in all circumstances. As the boys began to grow and test their boundaries, so did the two thousand students I had pledged to hold accountable. This assignment was a personal gift for me as I became in tune with the tactics. I saw their job was to push their boundaries as hard as they could. I also recognized someone always needed to be in charge and draw the line.

Life as an assistant principal wasn't all about the students. I also needed to learn to maneuver a course with teachers, parents, and a school district filled with politics. This is when the analytical strategies I had learned on the chessboard began to kick in; I needed to have a back-up plan for every move I made, fully document every incident, and be prepared to speak and back up *my truth* at all times.

In a leadership position, the only way to survive was to be transparent and keep a consistent course for all to see. If you were inconsistent in any way, especially when you delivered consequences, you had no hope of people seeing that you had a steady course. If you made exceptions for *one* you might have to make exceptions for *all*.

Three years at a middle school in a leadership capacity earned me my first principal position. *I had no idea what I was walking into.* My destination was an elementary school located in a gang area. The previous principal had recently been fired for not expelling a student who had come to school brandishing a knife.

Originally, the school had been established at the end of a small cul-de-sac in a field across from a river. Somehow, it had become the largest elementary school in the district with 965 students and no assistant principal. *I was walking into a lion's den.*

My first meeting with the teachers revealed that they were not ready for the shifts ahead. The new superintendent had responded with a Zero Tolerance Policy to the parents who were concerned about the growing violence in their schools. Fighting, threatening, or intimidation would earn a suspension. Three strikes would lead to expulsion. During my first year, I had over one hundred suspensions and twenty expulsions. My number one job was to set up a safe campus.

At the same time, the State of California instituted teaching standards that were measured by student academic performance and would become the basis for the school's state ranking.

"This may not be the cruise you signed up for, but it is the one we are on," I said to the staff at our first meeting. I was a sailor and I had models and pictures of sailboats all over my office. I had a plaque that one of the teachers had gifted me which read, *When you can't change the direction of the wind, adjust your sails.* On the top of my office door was a brass plaque that read *Wheel House* and a sign I placed on the door when I left the office read *Gone Sailing.*

The superintendent gave talks each week at leadership meetings, saying we needed to move our scores each year to the next safe harbor. I began to imagine myself as the captain of a large brigantine ship sailing up the California coast. The staff playfully began calling me Captain Bligh, but over the years they shortened it to Captain. I never lost sight of my main job—I was responsible for all souls on board.

Some say hell is on earth and that first year, I truly believed it was. My primary goal was to build a safety net around the campus. Every day, I had files of students sent to my office for fights or for bringing paraphernalia to school. Plus, I was required to observe and evaluate forty-five teachers every two years.

The parents were also challenging. The school had scheduled a Halloween carnival for the Friday night before the thirty-first. I had booked security, but the event was overrun with drunk parents wearing gang colors. Predictably, fights broke out. Afterwards, when the Parent-Teacher Organization (PTO) parents took the proceeds from the carnival off campus to count the money, I knew I had bigger issues on my hands. I called them the next day, asking them to return with the money.

"Are you accusing us of doing something illegal?" said the president of the PTO.

"I can't say what has been done here. You took the proceeds that belong to the students off this campus to be counted somewhere else. How much money do you have in the bag now?"

"Twenty-five hundred dollars." I knew the school up the road had made eight thousand dollars in one evening.

"It sounds a little short to me," I said.

"Listen," said one mother. "This is none of your business."

"None of my business? I'm the principal of this school and that money is for the students only and I need to ensure that."

"No, you're wrong. We are the PTO and we are a separate entity; you have no jurisdiction over us."

I found out they had a point when I asked the school's Resource Officer. So, I asked them to bring the remaining monies to the school secretary, who put it in the school's safe. Then I asked for their resignations. *I was in the wild west.*

One afternoon, our night custodian told me he was afraid to stay and clean the school on Friday nights. "The local members of the neighborhood gang are beginning to meet on the campus by the tables in the outside eating area."

"Okay, what time do they usually get here?" I asked.

"About seven, after dark," said Bob. He was scheduled to work till ten.

"Okay, I'll stay. I want to talk to them first," I said. I don't know what I was thinking, but I wanted to give them a heads-up before I involved the police.

Bob and I walked up to the group of six and Bob made introductions.

"Listen, you guys, you need to move your group to another spot, you can't be meeting on a public school campus at night. This is a safe community zone," I said.

"Well, we have nowhere else that is safe to meet either. The Crips know where we live and this is out of their view."

"So, what happens when the word gets out you're meeting here? Are we going to have a gang war here, where you once went to school? Listen, I respect all people and I'm showing you respect right now. I'm out here talking to you before I call the police—this is called a heads-up. Now, I'm turning around and going inside. If you are still here in ten minutes, I'm calling them. Understood?"

Bob called me ten minutes later on the two-way radio, "I don't know how you did it, but they're gone." *That was lucky.* The fathers in the neighborhood began referring to me as "the He-She." I took that to mean I was the boss.

I felt bad for the staff, as I had had no time that first year to build the level of trust needed to move things forward in a school. So, they resorted to writing petitions with signatures about things they wanted changed and served me the envelope of petitions on the last day of school.

I apologized to them immediately. "Listen, I'm very sorry I haven't been able to listen and value your thoughts this year. That was not my intention. I recognize that schools don't move forward unless we are all doing the work together. It is going to take every idea and hundreds of strategies to find the answers. I will be putting together task force teams to help solve these and the many more problems that are ahead. Please join the teams, I need all the help I can get."

I went back to my office, read through the petitions, and had a good cry. It would have been easy to quit at that point, but that wasn't why I was there in that place and time. I was there to make a difference. *It is funny—when the challenging moments come, you recognize your choices to rise up and meet them are part of the fabric of your destiny.*

Besides, I would never forgive myself if I didn't try. I was alone in that office; it was up to me. That is where the grit, patience, and resilience needed to start. I had a long talk with myself that night and when I walked to my car, I had determined I was in this journey for the long term.

The next year, we established task forces and leadership teams to address the issues on their petitions and dozens more that we needed to tackle to boost our low California state school performance ranking.

At the beginning of our second year, during one of our first staff meetings I said, "Well, the main advantage of being one of the lowest is we have nowhere to go but up."

More than half of our students were second-language learners. "Imagine taking that test when you can't even figure out what it is asking you. Let's help them be successful. Our students are smart and we need to let them know it."

We worked on goals to start an aggressive Accelerated Reading program (with recognition and rewards for students and teachers) and strengthen our writing program with daily writing exercises and vocabulary-building games. We became a team to be reckoned with. In two short years, we gained over a hundred points. We still had a long way to go, so we brought in computer programs for those students who still had learning gaps and added more time and programs for math.

I was often quoted as saying, "It is what it is," and "All's well that ends well." I used them most days.

After six years of diligent work, we were recognized by the State for having one of the highest scores and were awarded the California Distinguished School Award. *It was such an exciting time for everyone.*

They called us "the little school that could." Even Governor Arnold Schwarzenegger came down to our little village of disintegrating portable classrooms to deliver a state address from our library. He greeted the students with pride in their achievements and gave a pep talk, "You know, I didn't get to be an actor or a governor without hard work. I, too, came to this country as an immigrant, not speaking a word of English."

Yes, many of our journeys are challenging and convoluted. We often want to quit but don't because the secret sauce for the spice of life is buried in the challenge. Keeping a steady course is never easy—you may need to adjust it each and every day while that fierce wind blows.

A wise man once told me, "It is a fool who thinks he is on a quest to seek happiness. Happiness isn't a prize that is sought and won, it is that warm, satisfying feeling we get at the end of every day after we tried our best and surrounded our life with the warmth of loved ones."

My parting gift to the students I teach and to friends who are moving on is a brass-encased compass. It always comes with a note or is engraved with *Always follow your True North*.

The last group of fourth-grade students I gave it to weren't sure what a compass was. We went outside and I asked, "What do we use a compass for?" One student knew that people and sailors used it for direction, but they had no idea how to use one. So I asked, "Where is east?" After a little discussion, one student pointed a finger, "It's over there, where the sun rises."

"Great, so before we open the brass top of the compass, where is north?" I had them stand up and point, and about half pointed in the direction of north.

"North is important because the compass is designed to point to the magnetic north." After we spent a day on orienteering with our new tool, we got into a metaphorical discussion about how each of them had a True North and they were the only ones who would truly know where their compass pointed. I told them to always follow what they knew would fulfill their heart and soul and extend their happiness to others.

"Never lose this compass. If you feel lost, just open it and ask yourself, *Where is my True North*? And you'll find it."

The next year, I was walking down the hall of the school and one of the students glanced over and said out loud, "I haven't lost my compass yet, Miss."

"I'm so glad to hear that. Keep it close and you will never lose your way. It's magic."

So back to the question I asked myself that day on the sailboat: the answer is, I stood alone at the helm of a boat at age sixty-two because I was an adventurer. I had several directional pulls in my life, but this one had a greater impact on my life than any of the others. It didn't allow me to be anchored; I always needed to be looking for the new horizon.

Love can't always set us straight and, at its worst, it can leave us blindsided. Best to always love yourself—it can set you free to follow your True North and live your best happy life.

A New Jersey native, Georgia Faye flew off to travel the world in 1975 and found her True North by answering an advertisement for a teaching job in Sydney, Australia, to remedy the country's severe teacher shortage.

In her breakout novel *Down Under*, Georgia explores her introspective journey, from the choices she made in those early years, to her life's path as a single mother, and eventually the decision to live her life on a boat.

Georgia has lived in San Diego for over thirty years. She currently lives on a forty-year-old motor yacht. Her career in education for the last twenty-five years led her to be recognized through major awards for community and global development including Zero Waste programs, STEM school development, innovative farm-to-table programs, and two Distinguished School Awards, which ultimately earned her the title of Southern California's Principal of the Year.

Georgia is the proud mother of two beautiful sons and has six adorable grandchildren. She continues to pursue an adventurous life traveling the world and participating in international volunteer programs in faraway places such as Croatia, Greece, and West Kenya.

Although Georgia has been writing for years, she only recently published the novel *Down Under* after contributing a chapter in *The Pivot Project* anthology during the global pandemic. Her chapter "Navigating Happiness" was selected as the first chapter of the anthology to start the reader on a journey of short stories. Georgia is a member of the San Diego Writers and Editors Guild, the Writer Digest Guild, the Wild Atlantic Writers Association, the Authors Guild, and Romance Writers of America. To contact Georgia Faye email Info@MoonscapePress.com.

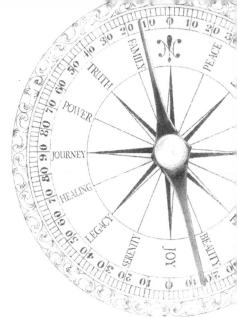

Embodied by Soul

Esthela Núñez Franco

Getting a mullet was not my idea, especially a week before immigrating to the United States. My godmother treated me to a new haircut and dress for the journey, briefly forgetting I was only ten years old and looked better in traditional long braids. She told me to be brave and happy and always remember my destiny to be an artist and a teacher.

I never saw her again. I experienced loss for the first time.

My mother and I were terrified of embarking on a journey to the United States without my father, but she was more terrified of a possible separation at the border crossing. Family members suggested that crossing the border in separate vehicles would be best and less conspicuous. When I saw my mother drive away, my heart bled in pain and ached with anger. I could not hide it, nor did I want to—I wanted my *mami*.

My only comfort was a harsh order to sit in the back seat and shut up. How can you stop a bleeding and angry heart when it refuses to listen? You quietly let it hurt until it cannot hurt anymore. Seeing my mother drive away was a form of torture I had never experienced before—it almost killed me. Almost. After reuniting with her two days later, the leftover pieces of my heart started a long healing process.

As a traditional Mexican woman, I have never left my mother's womb or my father's heart. I cannot abandon what is sacred, honorable, and true.

Our destination was Colorado and our first stop the city of Dallas, Texas. That city was my first impression of the United States of America, and I felt a sense of my new life. We arrived at night; I became immediately intrigued by the many lights and the number of buildings in the city center. Spending the night in an apartment was a new experience, starting with stepping on carpeted floors. Where was the tile? The sounds of America were different and scary at times during that first night. My mother never let me out of her sight; she kept her eyes on me in an almost animalistic and primitive manner. The next day, she and I saw a black person for the first time in our lives. He stepped out of the elevator, greeted us, and carried on. It felt great to see people from all backgrounds. America, indeed, was just like the television shows I watched, inclusive and welcoming to all people. My native country was and continues to be socially divided by the long-standing tradition of colorism (discrimination based on skin color) flowing through its veins. It is an unfortunate and cruel reality. As a new immigrant, I felt excited to be a new member of the American family, but quickly found out that my new family was not ready for me.

Not having the right clothes, money, or last name was a good enough reason for other kids to pick on me. Not speaking English in school made me vulnerable, an easy target for endless bullying accompanied by derogatory racial comments. To this day, I am not sure what some of the racial slurs meant, I just knew how they made me feel.

Every evening, I cried and begged my parents not to send me back the next day, but they always sent me back to fight a battle they were helpless to fight for me. Thinking back, I can only imagine what my mother must have felt but never showed. She taught me to be strong and my father taught me not to be afraid. The teachers who helped me through those moments have my most profound and eternal gratitude; their task had to be frustrating and complicated. (This was a time before English as a Second Language programs were in place.)

Occasionally, a ray of light would shine in the middle of my darkness. Being invited to a classmate's birthday party and tasting Neapolitan ice cream for the first time was the highlight of my ten-year-old life. I had never seen ice cream with three colors and flavors together. I can still taste each flavor when switching from vanilla to chocolate to strawberry, all in the same serving—it was crazy. Jennifer was my classmate's name; she was also a victim of bullying. I was the only guest at her party, held in her home, a camper trailer parked inside a junkyard. My mother dressed me in my best with new shoes completing the party outfit.

Jennifer's home and family introduced me to another America, one I never saw on television shows. Shortly after the birthday party, her family moved out of state. I never saw Jennifer again. She was my one and only friend.

Children can, indeed, be ruthless without realizing the consequences of their bullying actions. Choosing not to have many friends later in my life was greatly influenced by events during my formative years in school. During that difficult time, my parents stepped in as friends and protectors. They were and continue to be everything I needed.

It is said that children choose their parents; therefore, my parents were my destiny. For the most part, they were never able to help with schoolwork, attend school meetings or events, or provide college tuition. My parents taught me to love and respect the United States. At times, this was quite a task for a passionate, expressive, and delicate Mexican heart.

Never did I feel so out of place and out of my element. My school years were lonely and dark; I do not remember most events, only most feelings. I often dream of being back in that same school as an adult, struggling to find a classroom while desperately running around naked. Most people do not realize how influential high school is for teenagers. A positive or negative influence only changes the mark's shape; it does not alter the mark itself. Today's high school students may have an even rougher time with bullying since social media platforms are available 24/7, identical to a news network. My advice to students going through similar circumstances is simple and straightforward: *This too shall pass.*

Destiny and luck had more macabre plans for me as a young adult—a failed marriage immediately after high school and the start of my rare autoimmune disease. This time, my heart and I separated. I have difficulty remembering my twenties too. No details are readily available, just feelings of being lost and inadequate.

The less-macabre plans destiny and luck had in mind for me include a decision to be the first person in my family to go to college. Becoming a college graduate was the best gift I could give my parents. Walking down the stairs wearing my cap and gown to greet my father is a memory I do not forget.

Having only a third-grade education, my parents always felt they never gave me enough. I express my appreciation by devoting my adult life to help them. Becoming a parent of senior citizens was never my plan; it was my destiny. Luck made sure I got a little break here and there. By now, I was used to not having a normal life; taking care of parents was now just part of the abnormal mix. Destiny and luck made sure I had what I needed. Frequently, help came in odd and unusual ways such as random assistance from perfect strangers or pure, unadulterated luck manifestation such as finding money on the street that I desperately needed to pay my parents' mortgage.

After college, I was the grand marshal in the parade of professional accomplishments and success. Money was never the measurement for my success, only feelings and emotions. The meaning of success is different for everyone who wishes to embark on the complicated journey to find and conquer it.

By then, I knew what I was looking for and how to recognize it. It tasted good and smelled wonderful, like a freshly baked cake flooded in cream cheese frosting served with Neapolitan ice cream. I knew it when I tasted it and was unable to stop eating it.

Success for me never meant stepping on or taking advantage of others. It meant being of service to others in a humble manner with zero expectations. Nobody needs to know what I do for others except me.

My commitment to growth does not guarantee more success; it guarantees and strengthens my commitment to deeper learning.

I remember those who helped or hurt me in the same manner with consistent feelings of best wishes.

And I never forget to fail forward with gratitude.

I am not sure when my switch flipped to this new way of being—it had to be at the defeat of anger and pity. My strong and positive attitude stood at the bedside of my anger and pity, waiting patiently for them to die, never pushing or rushing because all things die when they are supposed to.

Life was great until, somewhere in my journey, I lost my Soul. I did not wake up one day to realize my Soul was missing. I never felt it leave or fade. I did not accidentally leave it in an airport or a restaurant during my many travels. Its loss may have been the result of a typical human error, but which error?

The truth is, you can only find something if you know it's lost. I did not know I had lost my Soul until I failed to find that something or someone inside of me. That's when I knew it was gone. Regardless of how much I looked, I found nothing. Every time I had an unsuccessful search, I was left swimming in an overwhelming pool of doubt and confusion that wanted to drown me. I swam in the deepest end of the pool, never reaching top or bottom. Exhausted, I begged to drown. It never happened.

It is horrible to lose your Soul and I do not wish that on anyone. Humans are not meant to be without a Soul; losing it means having a life full of nutrients without the benefit of absorbing nourishment. I kept missing the nourishment my body needed to survive and thrive.

My life was in a constant state of malnutrition and my door was wide open for diseases and enemies. Fear was my first visitor. It pretended to be a friend and an ally. It enjoyed confusing me by making me feel safe and guarded, and I believed it to be my savior and helper. But fear is full of lies and false promises.

After being governed by fear for decades, little pieces of myself began to retaliate and asked me to bring back their essence and reason for living. They demanded that my Soul be returned at once and in one piece. This retaliation came in the form of a rare autoimmune disease. As my body struggled to give me every possible symptom it could think of, my mind fell into a deep abyss of pity and victimization. My body's symptoms were signs that kept asking me and, at times, desperately begging me to find my Soul. My mind refused to help. It was weak, dark, and a casualty of depression.

Internally, life became unbearable. I promised myself I would find my Soul and bring it back. It was necessary, critical, and crucial for all of us—my Soul, Mind, Body, and Heart—to survive the disease. My Soul had to be found before time ran out.

I embarked on my journey, unwilling to stop and ask for directions; fear had me convinced I had to do this alone. My journey was long and laborious, many days lost, many days without direction. Occasionally, I would get help from other travelers who were also on a journey to find their Soul. I was comforted to know others were out there too, looking for something precious and unique. Many travelers shared their experiences and provided advice. Some had started their journey recently; others had been traveling for decades, if not centuries. I regretted not keeping safe and guarded, but it was too late for that—I kept going.

The feeling of losing hope was always present and ready to take center stage. This was an enemy who constantly taunted me by offering help, hoping I would accept it. I didn't want or need more enemies making an appearance; Soul had to be found. I kept walking, sprinting occasionally to gain more ground. Some days, I ran so fast I quickly ran out of breath and thought I would die. Other days, a brisk walk was fast enough and allowed for some rest.

One day, when I least expected it, I stumbled upon my Soul. At our first and quick encounter, following cordial small talk, we realized we had been looking for each other. It was that simple. At last, my Soul, Mind, Body, and Heart here together again.

The feeling of losing my Soul is similar to growing up in a foreign country. It is like a repetitive dream, waking up to different traditions, customs, food, lifestyle, and even fashion. Sleepless nights are complemented by awkward mornings full of confusion and never-ending feelings of wanting to go back home as soon as possible, full of regret that I moved to a strange country but unable to return to the comfort and security of my birthplace.

I never returned to my native country. Thinking back, it should not have mattered where my home or country was, as long as I had my Soul. In order to survive the awkwardness of a new country I had to say goodbye to having just one culture and begin weaving two dissimilar cultures together. This helped build a foundation for my new home.

Decades of being the mediator between two cultures had taken a toll on me. Once I fully surrendered to my Soul, I accepted the idea of going back to the basics of being human again; I suspect the last time I felt that way was back in kindergarten.

Out of curiosity, one day I asked my Soul what kept the rest of us together during its absence. Everyone got quiet to listen; then my Soul quietly suggested that something else kept the beat going. With the exchange of limited information, I knew there was more to come. My Soul's silence told me there was another important being responsible for keeping my Mind and Body together and ensuring my survival for years.

I had the habit of overshadowing my heart with my own self. I felt I was more intelligent than my heart. My Soul had to act as an intermediary to teach me how to respect and take care of my heart. During our first introduction, I could not make eye contact with it. I was shy and full of blushing. My heart was very seasoned and experienced and I was learning to walk and carry myself, yet I was in my forties. The meeting was intimidating but never degrading. I had so many questions for my heart, yet I couldn't verbalize them. Some things are best left unsaid; the power of silence is often underestimated.

A heart is very talented; when broken it maintains its beat. Not too long ago, my broken heart came back to help me heal. I know who brokered the first meeting—my Soul. I cannot preach that what worked for me will work for anyone else. I can only humbly advise anyone never to be afraid of his or her heart. I am no longer frightened of what lives inside of me. It is just me. I talk to my heart to know it better; after all, it desperately sought a relationship without ceasing.

Losing my son was a private and deep matter that I chose not to share with loved ones until fifteen years later. Carrying a secret in a broken heart is similar to capturing and keeping wildlife; some things are made to be wild and free. That was the idea during creation and evolution. It takes hard work to maintain a broken heart. It must be set free to run in the wilderness for healing. Its duty and strategy is to run as far away as possible, make a full circle, and come back to its human without ever skipping a beat.

When I shared my secret of losing my son with my family, my heart held my hand throughout the conversation and was there to comfort me afterward. My son deserved to be acknowledged by my family and honored by me by giving him a final resting place. My heart and I made all the arrangements. It stood by my side, never failing to provide healing on a wound that closed too soon. Soon after, I stopped hurting and healed from the inside out.

The relationship between my heart and me is relatively new. I am enjoying our honeymoon stage. Everything is new and exciting. Both of us suffer from separation anxiety when apart, and regular check-ins are required throughout the day. A relationship with my heart has been quite the adventure up to now; it is definitely not what I expected.

How did I find my Soul and embody it? Easy—I looked inside of me. Being embodied by Soul meant having the realization of who and what I really am—a human being. My Soul was there; it had never left. It had waited for me to start a relationship with and for myself.

Recognizing my own emotions and feelings was not done alone, but with someone special in my life. He helped me find my Soul, who later introduced me to my heart. Everything I am today is because of him—and I will leave it at that. With his help, I placed myself in front of the mirror and had a 360-degree look. It is the hardest thing I have done in my life. It felt worse than looking at myself in front of a mirror in a department store dressing room, which is horrifying enough.

Nevertheless, who decides which mirror to look at and who determines what looks good or not? The answer is short and straightforward—me. I tried on many outfits in life, some fit and others not so much. I found the ones that made me most comfortable and happy. Other outfits in life did not quite have the right fit; instead, they had the right feeling regardless of their look, brand, or make. Everything is relative; I had to find my relative.

My future, career, human relationships, goals, and life in general never made sense until I learned to start and carry on a deeper dialog with myself. Please think of how children have no problem getting to know themselves. They know what they like, love, or hate in the blink of an eye. They embrace and guard their souls as something precious and unique. They are not embarrassed by it or have any regrets for exposing it occasionally. Quite the contrary— children look for every opportunity to showcase their Soul. They are eager to introduce it to anyone open to meet it. They bring out their Soul to play and, when the game is over, they lay it down to sleep. Children's Souls have an inviting and contagious rhythm that makes children dance. I find myself feeling envious when children can freely express how they think without a filter or reason.

Defending their children, parents frequently say, "Please forgive them, they are just children." But are they just children? They are humans in their purest form. Bringing my team of Soul, Mind, Body, and Heart together again has brought me a step closer to being a human in my purest form. My Soul is the team lead who happily gives the stage to other members and thrives on seeing them develop, succeed, and learn. My Soul is supportive and full of wisdom. It is very modest in offering advice and is eager to hear ideas from my Mind, Body, and Heart. Soul is the team leader because it was present before the others were. It patiently waited for me, it's human.

Soul, Mind, Body, and Heart are a perfect team. They strive to win but happily accept losses with gratitude and dignity. There is no better teacher than a mistake that makes me fall flat on my face and no better lesson than to stand firm. The best part is having a great team accompany me in every journey of my life.

The embodiment of a Soul is available for every human in any country. My Soul would have caught up to me regardless of my country of origin or current residence. Souls do not care about birth certificates or passports. My Soul is omnipresent, in and around me. Once it has been identified, nobody wants to lose his or her Soul. It will be guarded and kept in the safest place, inside of us.

Why would someone want to miss the opportunity of becoming human again? Of being able to be humble, loving, of service, genuine, real, creative, and sincere? My Soul did not make me embrace two cultures; the two cultures embraced me with my Soul's permission and guidance.

While I wasted years trying to figure out who I was and in what direction I was going, all I needed to do was look inside and speak with my Soul. It was a time for me to wake up and smell me. No roses or coffee, there was nothing else important enough to smell. My Soul is very caring but occasionally it can have a mean streak and limited patience, just like any other being. When it gives up on giving me endless hints, it gently thumps me on the head. This is the only time getting thumped on feels comforting and familiar. Clear visions manifest, as comforting as going to back to my childhood home in my native country. My Soul reminds me that the location of my home is inside of me and never anywhere else. Everyone has a Soul, which means everyone has a home.

As an endless talker, I continue to question and debate with my Soul whether humans are driven by destiny or luck. Our debates get heated and intense, and usually end with me walking away like a toddler in the middle of a temper tantrum. My Soul is always right; it reminds me that I am a beneficiary of both destiny and luck. I think Soul tricks me at times and enjoys watching my reaction. It should not matter which came first, destiny or luck. What matters to me is their working relationship. What destiny did not give me, luck made up for it. I never win a debate against my Soul; I am not that intelligent, and I frequently get tangled in my own arguments. Certainly, any Soul gets to laugh at their human's stupidity.

I have learned a few things from my Soul, an excellent teacher. For instance, the same human experiences that bring us together, keep us apart. I learned that it is my duty to share my experiences to help others and break my heart open in the process. My heart has been cracked a few times but only broken once. There is no better therapy. A broken heart is open and ready to take in additional new experiences, emotions, and feelings.

Of course, not everything is Neapolitan ice cream and cream cheese cake in my life. I simply choose to look at life as my favorite dessert. I switched happiness from a feeling to a choice. This includes its definition, duration, intensity, and cause. I am in charge of my own happiness. Writing this piece makes me happy, so I do it. Other people, things, or places are not responsible for providing me with a daily happiness dose.

After deciding to be happy, I was blown away by the intense feeling of freedom and liberation that comes with making that choice, which is increasingly becoming one of my favorite things in life. Everyone who decides to make the choice to be happy should get ready. In my case, readiness has never been my forte; I tweak and adjust my happiness choices for a lesser blow.

Checking in with the responsible department is a priority. As a passionate and expressive Mexican woman, pleasure and responsibility play musical chairs in my mind. It can be difficult to balance family traditions and morals with the basic instincts and pleasures of being a grown and independent woman.

Generosity can become an uncontrollable force in my life. Learning to differentiate between giving more and being better is a daily challenge. At the end of the day, when I look deeper into the motives behind my generosity, I see and understand the justification and true reasons for giving and remind myself that giving is not about me.

Passions are filed in one of my mind's cabinets. They are well organized, in alphabetical order with colored tabs. I live and breathe passion. Over the years, I concluded and accepted that a passionate life is a lonely one. It is rare to find others who are quick to jump with me on the passion train departing every hour on the hour. My passion comes with energy, impulsion, esteem, and vision.

If I blow away with the freedom and liberation from choosing happiness, passion simply erases me off the map. There is not another way for me than living through my passion. It is not a hobby or pastime, a like or dislike. Passion was the material used during my creation. It is a sturdy and weather-resistant material that has stood the test of time, it is my cover and content. I cannot live without it and it does not live without me.

No, passion is not who I am; it is what I am made of. Occasionally, it calls for minor and cosmetic external and internal repairs. It is vital that I take care of it and maintain its upkeep. I cannot allow it to be destroyed or damaged or to decay due to simple carelessness.

It is great to see my passion again after all these years. Passion and I met each other at an early age—kindergarten, to be exact. Being expelled from kindergarten was not exactly what my parents planned for on my third day of class. The reason for my expulsion was excessive standing up in front of the chalkboard with a desire to teach the lesson. The name of the reason felt legal in nature—my desire to teach was too grand to keep inside my four-year-old body. Reading and writing at four years old and being freshly expelled gave me the green light to step into first grade. I can only thank my parents for making the right choice and accepting the teacher's recommendation. (My mother was the culprit in teaching me advanced academic skills early; she is my passion's godmother.)

Seeing beauty was the open door to my religion and spirituality in a simplistic and human way. Schedules of rituals or traditions are unnecessary and pointless in my life. I choose to walk in a path of constant meditation and reflection. No, that does not make me a zombie or a monk; however, it does have a slowing and calming effect. Sadly, so much beauty is missed when I forget to slow down, choose to look and not see, or hear and not listen. Beauty has always been present in the history of and before humanity. Evolution and creation had to be full of beauty. It would have been awesome to see it unfold; however, I think we all participate in witnessing evolution and creation every day. Beauty should be seen, felt, and loved in the most unconditional and forgiving way.

When people ask me to choose between religion or spirituality, my answer is neither and both at the same time. A strict Roman Catholic upbringing was not enough to change or make up my mind. My parents raise an eyebrow when I openly discuss other religions or various forms of spirituality during Sunday dinners. *I am sorry, Mom and Dad, not everyone is Catholic and Jesus didn't speak Latin!* I was forced to obey the motions and rituals of Catholicism while growing up and became a master of acting. With age, I replaced acting with respect.

Tolerance, acceptance, surrender, and just let it be, is my method for navigating through religion and spirituality. Both are omnipresent, in and around us, at every moment of our lives. I found the kind of religion and spirituality combination that worked for me. It does not have a label, method, or process; it just is. Ironically, this method also works in all aspects of life.

My story is not one of a successful immigrant or an unusual and extraordinary attainment of the American dream. It is just another story of a human who has been in the production department more than four decades. This is a story that matters only to me. The family may not understand it, and outsiders may not care.

It is about leaving the past behind and finding my Soul moving forward into the future. Picking up the pieces and gluing them back together, regardless of fit. It is about stripping all the paint and showing the gridlines of my plain canvas. Accepting and embracing all the even and uneven lines blending in harmony. It is about becoming human again. Every relationship is different. I can only write about the relationship with my Soul, Mind, Body, and Heart. Not all the pieces came together at once. In a way it is similar to any personal relationship. Everything takes time, but I want to tell you that it is never too late to find your Soul, Mind, Body, or Heart. They are not lost; they have never left you.

I now share my internal space with other beings. I am not be surprised or scared if they are rowdy and obnoxious tenants, they are the kindest beings you will meet. My only wish is the best for everyone else's relationships. I do not possess credentials to give advice, as I am only human. My message to you is to never lose hope in the journey.

At the age of ten Esthela Núñez Franco immigrated with her parents to the United States, where they made their home in Colorado. Born with passion running through her veins and an endless love of books, she learned to embrace life simply as a human. Her mother's intuition quickly identified her daughter's interests, motivating her to teach Esthela reading and writing at the young age of four years old. Esthela's advanced academic skills opened the floodgates to a lifelong dedication of extroverted personal expressionism in reading, writing, painting, and photography. Today, Esthela believes her life creates the best stories; she simply helps the process along by giving them a voice and acting as an intermediary and interpreter.

In her career, Esthela Núñez Franco uses her MBA to bring leadership and expertise to the ever-changing field of corporate human resources, using her gifts as a working professional by trade and an artist by birth. Esthela debuted as an author with the BreezyGirl book series, including the titles *BreezyGirl: A Day with Mom, Grandpa is Happy,* and *My Uncle Is Sick.* The strong message of family bonds nourished by endless loving support is the center of her creative yet peculiar book series.

Esthela's projects include additional children's books written in her native Spanish language. Her creativity occasionally steps aside, allowing her heart to break open and tell her story in a memoir, which she is in the throes of writing. She believes everyone has a story inside; some are just courageous enough to write it. Esthela considers her memoir the biggest challenge of her life where academic intelligence does not apply; only the presence of her heart and soul are necessary.

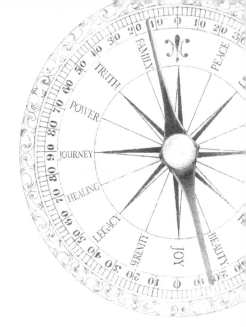

What the Dying Have Taught Me

Debra Zachau

There is a world between life and death that is active and compelling. I discovered it when I found myself witnessing the life people live inside this place and through their stories and ideas they have shared with me. My chapter is not focused on the living or the dead, but on the dying, the experiences that happen on the path from life to death. It's there I found my True North of knowing certain things *for sure*. To explore and teach what I've discovered in this space of awareness is what I bring to you today.

Like most people, I was born afraid to die, once I realized people did indeed stop living. A feeling of being under the gun grew. It haunted and followed me into every thought of the future or project I found myself doing. There seemed to be so much I wanted to do and experience. That *it* was the problem and *it* was annoying.

That being said, I knew the afterlife was real because up until I was about fifteen years old, I heard angelic choirs almost every day. The sound was unbelievable and undeniably otherworldly. It would begin low and as it got louder the superficial and frivolous noises of the house, store, party, church, or school I happened to be at got very quiet. It felt like when you go deaf just before your ears pop on a plane, but of course, it didn't hurt like that. Then, there the music would be, louder and more beautiful than the previous time. Always a little bit different and it would happen at different times of day, times of the week, and it never mattered if I was with people or alone.

My eyes would widen and quickly look around to see if anyone else was hearing what I was hearing. No one ever was; these concerts were designed for me and me alone. I'd turn my head trying to figure out which direction it was coming from, which direction would favor the music, but it was everywhere and in all places. I could hear every voice, word, and instrument in perfect pitch and harmony and I was standing inside of it evenly. The music was one sound, one unit, one effort, one perfect effort from many different sources. The song was always upbeat, happy, and celebratory. Hearing it made me brave and less uncomfortable being alone in the world. My wish is that every person has an opportunity to experience this while living because hearing it just once will erase all doubt that the afterlife is real. I promise.

Because of this I became interested in the psychic sciences and studied all of the different ways to divine the future and communicate with passed loved ones. My studies were constant and I integrated what I was learning into my regular work. I chose hairdressing as my trade and enjoyed building a like-minded clientele where we exchanged what we were both learning at the time during their hair service.

Death became my happy place, with all those sticky little threads that linger around a statement like that. Not just, one day you are alive and the next dead. There is plenty written about how to live and then communicate after death. But specifically, the space between healthy-minded and dementia. Between physically capable and then not. The time between having a voice and losing it. The land inside a coma. The person you knew so well who seems to have passed away before physically dying and another has taken their place.

This chapter is what I know to be true about what is happening during the in-between of being here (our "here" of understanding) and being over there, the never experienced. I've learned that this is a viable place, it is accessible, and I'll show you how to get there.

My True North story is one of how I became familiar with the in-between and have personally, with these discoveries, created firm footing regarding this mysterious place. I've discovered our friends and family members still have a voice and an active life with us while suspended both here and there. I want to share my experience so if perhaps you find yourself faced with a loved one inside this in-between you will be able to take advantage of the wisdom and grace it holds. I'm hoping you won't feel as lost or alone during this time. That you may find comfort through this information. You *can* hear them. They *can* hear you.

Life changes like these, when a loved one's personality starts fading, can be so disarming. Because your loved one can feel and understand your emotional state, without words, my hope is you will find this reassuring so you can remain calm, centered, and compassionate.

You may become fearful watching your loved one slip into this new territory. Afraid for yourself, afraid the doctors don't know enough and that the Bible might not be true. What starts out as emotional discomfort gives way to anxiety, followed by panic and then despair. Your loved one will pick this up and mirror it back to you, which makes this challenge harder.

Their life is richer than they may be showing on the outside and except for a few adverse impulses, they are, for the most part, not afraid. Most souls go in and out of awareness of their condition but will feel much more comfortable in the moment if their physical body is comfortable. If perhaps the elastic is too tight on a sensitive wrist or ankle, this alone can shift them into anger or becoming combative because the uncomfortable sensation tethers them to the day, the hour, and the reality of the situation.

Here is a bit of my journey that I now know to be true.

In 2003, after twenty-five years of integrating spiritual principles into my daily work life, the time came to say goodbye to Seattle, friends, family, and co-workers. I had lived in one place for so many years that now I wanted to see new places and challenge myself to a big change. Deliberately choosing a small town in southern California for my new beginning. Underestimating the cost of living in such a popular place and finding myself losing my financial stability soon after moving. I needed to find work much faster than planned but couldn't bring myself to do hairdressing inside a salon again. As much as I love the occupation I simply couldn't imagine standing behind a chair trapped inside the smell of chemicals when every day the sun was shining outside.

As an alternative, I decided to work as a mobile hairdresser through several hospice agencies in my area. They were always looking for a licensed pro to go into care facilities large and small serving those who could no longer leave home for services. To be clear, family members would ask their hospice workers if they knew of anyone who could come in and do hair at the bedside. The hospice workers would give them my name, and then we'd schedule an appointment. I worked on referral *through* hospice but didn't work *for* hospice. I was independent and my education about the dying was about to begin.

This was a wonderful work path for me. I was anxious to know more about end-of-life experiences as well as provide a much-needed service. Not to mention the benefits of being able to move around in the fresh air while working couldn't have been a better fit.

I met people in all stages of transition but learned a very important fact: Hospice is not necessarily the end of the line or an indication that death is imminent. Of course, as with all clients signing up for hospice care, the understanding was that the patient had six months or less to live. Many times, however, once a person was taken off all life-sustaining medications like high blood pressure meds or medication for cholesterol and put on comfort medication, they would get better and move off of hospice. I visited the same clients for years and years who I thought originally had only a short time to live. That was one of the best lessons I learned about this trying time inside families. Always remember, just because your loved one goes on hospice doesn't necessarily mean they will pass away within six months. Once they feel better emotionally their bodies can rally.

Some of my clients would have bodies failing and minds intact while others would have the opposite be true. It didn't matter what stage they were experiencing; having someone new come in every other month to do their hair was a refreshing delight. Both patient and caregiver seemed to enjoy the efforts and accommodations I made. My visit broke up an otherwise mundane day.

I learned so much about the process of dying and the important conversations between loved ones. I learned that for the dying, the distance between what is important, and what isn't, is shortened somehow because all of it matters. My client has surrendered their titles and is no longer a mother, a wife, a banker, a brother; they are the dying. New and profound emotions create a tension that my very ordinary service seemed to smooth. That haircut. That simple act brings a pause to a tiresome situation. The dying, if able, will recite a history of their hairstyles throughout their life. Such as remembering the day they asked their stylist for something new and the reactions of friends and family and how happy it made them. The family members relax in the joy of seeing their loved one look and act like themselves again.

The living, on the other hand, are processing something they may only experience once outside of themselves and the situation can feel quite profound. It makes everything else in their lives pale in comparison. People tend to release tiresome people, places, and situations and prioritize differently. Again, when realizing mortality small issues seem to matter more. It becomes easier to cut loose people and events that irritate on a day-to-day basis. People find themselves choosing to align and lean into situations that will bring more love and comfort.

Anyone who witnesses a process towards death needs to understand that each is unique and special. But more importantly, the experience will magnify a healthy person's focus on what needs to be done before they too need to surrender their own titles and become the dying.

My clients introduced me to this in-between world most every time I visited. They would point out people in the room and tell me how they're related and any history they had had with them. They would only be able to see and interact with this visitor if they were leaning into that world. If perhaps a living family member or caregiver mentioned that the person the client was referring to had already passed away the client would usually get quiet about it but that didn't mean the visitor had left. Usually, the rest of the family would step away while I worked, taking advantage of the break from responsibility. After they left I would encourage my client to tell me more about the one who was visiting and as they talked and as they leaned into that world I was able to see and hear them as well. It was through my client I was able to have the same experiences at the same time.

Like many people, I'm sensitive to the energy around me. Everyone has this ability to enter a room and get a feeling or impression of a spirit who may be there. But it was when I discovered I could piggyback onto a client's vision that the real fun began! They would say for example their sister (who was in spirit) was there and I would look to the corner they were facing and was able to see different images in my mind's eye. I would test myself and ask my client if the visitor had brown hair and was wearing a red dress, for example, and get really excited when I was correct. Yes, there is so much more going on between the living and the world of spirit.

One experience I had was with a gentleman who was very uncomfortable in his body but needed a haircut. He lived in a spacious private home with many residents. There was a very large bathroom with a large mirror. He was able to come in with his walker and sit facing the mirror, just like in a real salon. This man was short-tempered due to the amount of pain he was in. I asked him how he would like his hair and he just said, "Off." I laughed and put the cape around him and started with the clippers.

Every so often he would smile and chuckle without reason. I wondered if we were being visited by the other side. At that particular moment, I couldn't pick up on anyone because I was concentrating on his haircut. He was jumping around sharply when he laughed, and I didn't want to make a mistake. This guy was a completely different personality than the man who first sat down.

I asked, "What's so funny?" and he said, "That little girl is watching your every move; it's so cute and funny. Whenever you take a snip she gets her eyes really close, like between you and the scissors to see every little thing." I tried to tap into this little girl's spirit but couldn't. The task at hand needed too much of my attention and I couldn't relax enough. I finally asked, "Who is she?" He surprised me by saying, "How would I know, she came in with you! I watched her tagging behind you when you first came into the house and she hasn't left your side since!" So I knew I had a little friend keeping me company that day. It wasn't until later that night when I was alone in a quiet room that I was able to chat with this sweet and funny little spirit. Of course, because she brought so much joy to a man in such pain I invited her to tag along with me anytime.

Some visits were more profound than others and this next one really changed my life. It solidified a True North for me. It created firm footing in my belief in the unseen world. I was called to a huge private home facility where there was the main house in the front of the property and a smaller one in the back. Entering the first house the aroma of a hot lunch being prepared in the nearby kitchen was hard to miss. Walking through I saw the kitchen overlooked a large dining table being set for everyone to gather. The woman who was obviously in charge greeted me through a column of steam, asking if I was there to see Greta for her hair. I said yes and she pointed past the dining room table and through the sliding glass door towards the second house.

The big cement patio gave way to a wide walkway leading to another house. The surface had enough texture not to be slippery if wet but made walkers and wheelchairs easy to move. A few small patches of grass along with some colorful flowers flanked the path. The attention to detail was quite impressive.

I entered the second, smaller house through another sliding glass door that went right into the living room. A tall, slender well-groomed man sitting in a wheelchair with his back facing me turned and nodded at me. I smiled, said hello, and called out for Greta. Her caregiver came around the corner and waved me back to one of the bedrooms. She had just finished preparing Greta with her hair still damp from her shower. She was sitting in her wheelchair looking forward to the pampering. The caregiver mentioned that lunch would be ready in about thirty minutes and as she was dashing out the door I assured her Greta would be ready.

We had a wonderful chat as I trimmed, dried, and curled Greta's hair. When I finished I positioned the mirror so she could see how beautiful she looked, and Greta smiled and nodded. I rolled Greta's wheelchair out of the bedroom and down the hall, stopping to take in the approving thumbs-up from the man in the living room, and we rolled outside, down the path, and into the dining room where everyone cheered her arrival. Compliments rang out from all angles as I positioned Greta at her spot at the table. Due to the number of empty seats, I could tell almost everyone was there. The food was being served and I ran back to the other house to pack up my equipment.

I walked past the man still alone in the living room to quickly throw all my tools and towels into my bag and came back out to the living room. The house was empty of everyone, it was just him and me. I certainly wasn't going to leave him there. I asked him if he would like me to take him to lunch and he motioned me off with a wave and said while chuckling, "They'll come to get me when they're ready, or when they miss me." I laughed and sat down on the small sofa to his right and said, "I'll wait with you then." He shrugged his shoulders as if to say, "Suit yourself." I introduced myself while noticing how comfortable he looked in the wheelchair. I said, "Sitting in one is better than trying to get up and out of a deep sofa." He said his name was Mr. K. and wholeheartedly agreed. I told him how in one house I grabbed an empty wheelchair and had a little race to the dining room, noting how bad of a driver I was. He laughed and said, "Practice makes perfect." "I totally agree," I replied.

We spent the next ten minutes or so talking about his life and family before a caregiver came in to wheel him to lunch. I followed and stopped in the kitchen to compliment the cook on how wonderful the food looked and smelled as well as how as orderly and festive the place was.

I mentioned to her while tipping my head towards Mr. K., "What a nice conversation I had with him." She looked at me then back to him and said, "You mean you talked to Mr. K.?" I said, "Yes! He told me all about being a pilot in Vietnam, two tours, then opening up his own successful business and how he enjoyed flying privately until his stroke. He then talked about his grandchildren a bit." (I remember thinking at the time, when he mentioned having a stroke, that it was strange that his body had none of the normal signs of one. But I also knew that some recover quite well, so brushed it off.)

The stunned caregiver looked me in the eye, hardly breathing, and said, "Mr. K. can't speak. He lost his ability to speak or converse in any way, even with facial expressions, during his last stroke. How do you know his history?" she asked. "Are you a friend of the family?" "No," I said while looking back over to Mr. K. and, to my surprise, saw him slumped over to one side, a different man altogether. He needed someone to feed him yet just a few minutes before he was casually moving his shoulders and arms, sitting upright and talking without any disability.

Stunned, I felt my heart start to beat fast as the reality of what just happened began to overwhelm me. I just had a profound experience that I couldn't explain. I dismissed the query, saying I had to run to my next appointment. I drove away from the house and parked in the shade a few blocks away. I needed to process what had just happened. Mr. K. was relaxed in his chair and his arms were animated for his stories. He smiled and seemed so happy to tell me everything. It wasn't as if I had read the mind of a catatonic person propped up in a wheelchair. I had just had a conversation with a man, like you and me, viable and capable. He wasn't one of my clients that day but *was* the only one in the house who seemed absolutely normal, a person who just found sitting in a wheelchair more comfortable than a sofa.

I felt spirit close to me that day as I was granted quite a blessing to witness such a miracle. Since then I don't fully trust what my eyes see but remain open to all things. Would I have had that experience if someone told me, before meeting him, that he had had a catastrophic stroke that prohibited all levels of expression? I don't believe I would have. If someone had informed me I wouldn't have that portion of my brain open to the possibility of conversation. There would have been no room in my reality for this experience. I'm so happy I didn't have anything blocking this miracle from happening.

From that day I moved inward with my training knowing that to witness miracles you have to dismiss all opinions, biases, and assumptions. You need to empty your mind so there are no preconceived ideas and feel lifted to what I call a clean room filled with good company. The company of angels. In this place (inside your imagination) there are no demands to feel or say anything. Miracles are our inheritance and if we learn to live life through a novice's heart we can experience them often.

What does living with a novice's heart mean? When you don't think the words *should* and *shouldn't*. And by contrast, you don't have wishes or longings either. You position yourself in-between what should be and what is wished for. That's the place, for example, where you don't have an opinion about which flavor of ice cream is available to you or longing for a certain taste, you're just really happy there's ice cream. It's like living like a kid, when anything is possible.

If our minds are open without assumptions and especially expectations, there are so many miracles available to witness. I promised to teach you how to experience the wonderful and informative world behind the veil. These techniques can be used when wanting to get in touch with someone alive but not mentally available as well as those who have passed away.

This is harder to do if you have anything on a physical level that is pinching or shouting at you. For instance, if you have a headache or if you can't find a comfortable position to sit in. You can lie down as long as you're comfortable physically. If you are in a place with a lot of noise, consider going into the quiet space of your car.

If perhaps your loved one is troubled, angry, abrasive, shouting, or aggressive, you need to be able to secure their safety and move into a non-emotional place in your heart. Remember the condition is affecting a certain part of their brain at the moment. What you want to discover is if there is something on a physical level that you can take away or fix to make them more comfortable. They can't express their feelings or tell you what they need; your loved one is going to talk to you through your body sensations.

Do a quick self-assessment of the temperature of the space you're in and make sure none of your clothes are binding. Start asking your angels to show, through your body, what your loved one might be feeling. Something that might be provoking this behavior. Then wait. Take a deep breath and close your eyes. You may have a random itch you want to scratch, which is fine, but if that itch is at the same spot on your body and doesn't let up this could very well be the bridge of communication you have been hoping for. Sit a bit longer; do you notice hunger, thirst, or is there a tightness around your wrist or ankle? Spirit will show you on your own body if there is something problematic affecting your loved one physically that may very well be the source of the challenging behavior. Go back in and check those areas spirit highlighted to see if there is a bit of tubing or rough cloth rubbing there. Spirit will communicate and you can be sure about the information if you first start your discovery session in comfort yourself. Then act on the information.

I once had a combative client and quickly quieted my mind and asked spirit for help. Almost immediately my left foot started feeling like my shoe was too tight. I lifted my client's pant leg and found her ankle was swelling. Thinking this was the reason for the challenging behavior, we propped her leg up and the caregiver started massaging it. The client calmed right down and the swelling went down as well. I wouldn't have thought to check if I hadn't been given that sensation myself.

I didn't have to get quiet at all in a little different experience with a client who was angry and lashing out. I discovered if I stayed out of her sight in every way I could comb and cut her hair without triggering her temper. I never stood at her side or in front; I did the entire haircut standing behind her. Our second appointment, however, standing behind her and cutting didn't work. I looked around the room through *her* eyes and saw my reflection in the TV screen. We simply turned the TV on and her anger went away. If that hadn't resolved the situation I would have continued to look behind her eyes with her mindset until I found the source of her being able to see me. A mirror or window even. Remaining open and clear along with taking a quick mental assessment of my own body may point to or show me the reasons for the anger.

I'm not saying this worked every time I found myself with a combative client. Sometimes it's just the wrong time of day and I choose to schedule a return visit at another time. Being flexible is very important when serving this clientele. And my heart goes out to all caregivers who are devoted to the welfare of their loved ones struggling with these types of conditions.

When communicating with loved ones in a coma or certain kinds of dementia you do the same thing as with conscious people but remember one major difference: You cannot let yourself slip into feeling pity for them or feeling sad for yourself regarding their situation. This is easier said than done, I know, but having those feelings will block communication with them. Everyone fears being incapacitated. Try hard not to judge the situation or feel sorry for yourself and others while you are asking to communicate.

To start the conversation, get comfortable and empty your mind as mentioned above. When you can get quiet enough you will learn the difference between having a thought of your own and experiencing the thoughts of another. There's a definite feeling and shift that happens when a thought is placed in your mind from the outside. There is a huge amount of understanding that happens when you notice this difference. One sentence of thought coming into your mind from the outside carries a paragraph of information. I know that sounds confusing but stick with me. Remember the story about the angelic choir? One event carried many sensations. One thought coming into your mind from spirit or your passed loved one, even if it only has two understandable words, will transfer a lot of understanding. Like a miracle.

It happens more often than you think because humans *were born with this ability* but have turned it off for so long. Experiencing it once is all you need to trust the information to be true and then you can do it again and again.

One of the ways you can tell a thought isn't your own is when there isn't a story hooked to it. Tapping into the place your loved one is may feel like a dream. A bit fragmented. They don't know you can see what they see yet. Ask spirit to set up a meeting between you and your loved one. Again, try hard not to have deep emotions of sadness or imagining your loved one filled with frustration. The conversations will be soft and slow in the beginning. The words might be missed and drowned out through the volume of strong feelings. Don't look to your loved one to comfort you in your sadness as they are experiencing a world that has them relaxed and centered within themselves. Be mindful of body sensations so you can catch possible physical problems that can develop when someone is in bed or sitting for extended periods. Skin can become thin in places and you may sense they need to be turned or need padding to keep them comfortable. Enter this experience as an observer; it is through this state so much is revealed.

Once a person has completely passed away you can bring more of your own feelings and emotions into the conversations. Be aware we take our personalities with us to the other side so if your Uncle Pete loved boxing he most likely still loves boxing on the other side. Same with any prejudices and strong preferences he may have voiced while he was alive. We not only have the freedom of choice here, we have it after we die as well. One of my recent mediumship readings came with a unique sign near the end of our conversation. I said, "Your father's sign for you is horses running." She started to cry and said, "My dad loved the track!" I told her she wouldn't have to go to the track for the sign; it will come to her in some shape or form. This conversation just happened so she hasn't shared with me yet what sign appeared but it will. They always come through. For her, a sign will most likely be in the form of a painting, a magazine, or someone talking about horse racing over the radio.

Your passed-on loved ones are always interested in your well-being and comfort. If you need them, call for them, clear your mind, and put into practice everything above. Understand that you can communicate with the other side. Move into seeing life through the observer portion of your mind, relax your body and ask to have a word or two with someone you love. They will be there. I promise.

I encourage anyone interested in this topic to enjoy the fun of information gathering and actual direct communication. You can hire a talented medium of course. But know that there is a world you can visit on your own. Open your mind to the possibility your loved ones will be happy to show you around their new corner of the world. Inside your quiet moments open your mind and ask for undeniable signs that they are with you. That sign can be a butterfly, dragonfly, or hummingbird coming close, likely inches from your eyes. The reason small birds and insects are common signs is because souls in spirit can influence their flight so easy. But if trust is still challenged go ahead and ask for an undeniable sign: Your mother's name on the license plate on the car stopped in front of you. A call from a mutual friend you haven't heard from in years. Or a letter written before their death that finds its way into your hands. You don't have to know what the sign will be, just be open for one. There's more going on behind the scenes on your behalf than you think. Being in the game of life is tough and so many on the other side remember and want to help and guide. I am here for you as well.

In deep respect for your path,
Debra

"By understanding who you are at soul level, you can quickly manifest wealth, love, fulfillment, and contentment."

—Debra Zachau

A spiritual teacher, tarot reader, author, and speaker, Debra Zachau teaches many modalities of higher consciousness and holds classes for those who wish to pursue their dreams of serving the world through a career in metaphysics. As a popular speaker and entertainer who hosts mediumship circles, Debra is a master of tarot and a certified Soul Realignment practitioner providing services for those who want to go deeper into who they are at a soul level. She facilitates positive ways a person can live life through their most authentic self.

Debra has performed at large corporate events and entertained audiences, speaking on a wide range of topics. She is dedicated to her international clientele and supports them on a daily basis as a spiritual advisor.

Debra has developed an online training program for everyday people who have an interest in self-awareness and discovery using their own unique talents. This program helps participants answer questions and creates confidence for professionals seeking personal development and success. By learning how to tap into the information held in the higher ranges of consciousness, one can navigate personal challenges and turn those skills into serving others.

Debra makes her home in North San Diego County and travels to speak to audiences nationwide. She has been a guest on the "All Spirit Driven" radio show with Cheryln Peavler and "Animal World" with Martha Norwalk.

Visit Debra's website at www.debrazachau.com for details on how you can build a new life's work in the metaphysics world. To learn more about tarot, click on the online course Learn Tarot Once and For All.

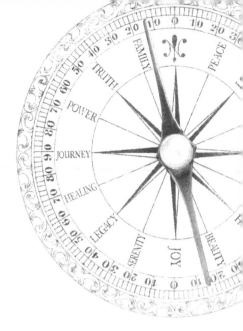

Dirty South vs. the True North!

Kirby Monestime

It's been said that the apple doesn't fall too far from the tree. Well, in some cases that is very true. In other cases, not so much. I believe each apple has the potential to fall as far from the tree as it really wants to because it has the ability to create its own consciousness, value, and belief system. It's about making the choice to do so.

Maybe that is part of this True North theory? What I do know with a great amount of certainty is the tree (my parents) was loving and nurturing and did the best it could to keep its apples (us kids) happy, safe, and well taken care of.

Growing up one of five kids was so much fun (at times). I'll never forget the seven of us crammed in our family car during the four-hour drives (or eight hours, depending on how bad Dad got lost) to Mrs. Benner's farm in Pennsylvania. Or the occasional throw your baby brother down the basement stairs or push your sister into the bathtub and hit her with your toy drill when she claimed Dad gave her permission to wear his new jacket when really, we know Mom gave me that same permission. All of that to say that while my childhood was filled with all of these fun, family-oriented memories, there was also pain and struggle.

All of those fond times I can look back on and chuckle a bit. They make for great memories as an adult. All memories I wouldn't want to give up. Those memories have helped form part of who I am today. A little bossy, strong minded, insistent, and the list goes on.

Being the first-born son is tough enough. Being the first-born gay son adds an extra layer of complexity to find that spot where you belong. You know, the spot where you know you have earned respect based on your place in the family lineage. I struggled with that, not knowing where I belonged most of my childhood and teenage life. My frustration and insecurity fueled fights with my brothers. During all those times I tried to assert my manhood. Did I even believe that manhood was there within myself? Sometimes, but not enough. What does "manhood" actually look like? Is there any such thing?

I remember feeling confused about my sexuality as a child. I liked girls, even had some huge crushes, and dated a few here and there. Sometimes I would watch a show or movie and find the women or females to be attractive and other times I would find the males to be attractive. Talk about confusing! It was painful to struggle with something like that in the silence of your own mind. My best friend Michelle—who I love dearly and who has been my rock for many years—says she knew I was gay in kindergarten. I oftentimes think, *I didn't even know what the hell gay really meant until I was in my teenage years. How does that work?*

Growing up in a religious Haitian home, sexuality wasn't really something we talked about at the family dinner table. After all, when it was time for "the talk" about sex, my dad took me to the library, sat me down at one of the tables, placed a stack of books in front of me, and said, "We are not leaving until you read all of these." How could I ever talk about my inner feelings and emotions, let alone the fact that I felt different? How could I determine who I really was?

When it came to my dad, I remember feeling less loved specifically and relating it to that feeling of being different. After years of come-to-Jesus moments, I realized there is no true formula for love and have learned to appreciate the way he showed love. People repeat the patterns that they felt, saw, and were taught in their lives to others. By virtue of the fact that my dad worked two jobs just to ensure that we were fed on the daily, in hindsight that of course was proof that he loved me. Actually, that was an example of love at its finest. As a child, you don't think of those things, but now as an adult, I do.

Even though I turned out to be a success in terms of education and business, an uncomfortable feeling still visits me every once in a while, like an unwanted guest who doesn't leave when you want them to. Oh, and they brought your least-favorite dessert—insecurity.

I guess in a sense, I am thankful for that insecurity. It challenges me to do one scary thing each day. I don't think that house guest is moving out any time soon, but it's taking more and more vacations lately and only comes home every once in a while. In other words, I am less impacted as each day goes by with that feeling of insecurity. I am learning to recognize when insecurity is trying to rear its ugly head. I breathe in, I breathe out and remember it's part of that thing called my "Dirty South," the alter ego of my True North. It's not who I am, it just shows up to remind me that I am amazing and have so much to offer this world. It shows up to remind me that I am headed toward my True North.

For those of you who have had to come out in a Christian home, I can definitely say I know how hard it was. If you grew up Pentecostal like I did, you may have been influenced to believe that the pastor can "pray the gay" out of you. You've also probably heard that "being gay is a choice." I heard that line once or twice. I remember asking my mom, "If being gay is a choice, then being straight must be a choice too, right? So, you actually are choosing not to sleep with women; it's not that you just don't have the inclination inside of you to do that. Right?" Needless to say, that didn't go over too well. In our home, you never talked back to Mom or Dad. I promise you, if being gay was a choice, I would've chosen the house, three kids, the white picket fence, and a fluffy dog named Candy Cane! At least, I would've then.

But through it all, I am learning so much about the psychology and psyche of people. In hindsight, what I am seeing now is that the fear of letting go of something you "should" believe is way greater than the fear of letting go of something you have been taught to be true your whole life. People grab on to an idea and don't let it go because they are afraid if they allow themselves to fluctuate on that idea, it will dismantle their entire belief system, the system they were taught to believe their entire lives.

So—many people feel they must stick to their truth that being gay is a choice, like being black, male, or tall. I get to choose who I am and what makes me, me. This is where my True North starts to manifest itself. While I believe in God, and do so to my very core, I am choosing to live my life in the theory of love. Remember the commandment that God Himself said is the greatest of all commandments: "Love your neighbor as yourself." Your neighbor might be gay, handicapped, a different nationality, a criminal, or have a different political affiliation, but we are called to love them just like we should love ourselves. We are called to be humane. Regardless of race, creed, or sexual orientation, let's just love. For me, that is part of my True North.

The dirty south would be going back to a place where I felt insecure about who I am and who I love. In the land of the True North, you get to believe what you want and I get to believe what I want but for me, everyone deserves love. God offers it to all so why shouldn't we offer it to others? Here's a novel idea, stop worrying about how people are classified and condemning them for that and let's just remember to love each other. That's part of my True North philosophy.

When I was a teenager, we lost my childhood home to bankruptcy. It made me sad because it represented a flaw in life and the society we live in. See, my dad worked two jobs and my mom was a nurse (until she got pregnant with my little sister and ultimately got ill). They worked harder than anyone I know for a long time, but they just couldn't keep up.

Now, my guess is that part of it had to do with my dad's desire to be an entrepreneur or even to get rich quick; let's just say that wasn't his forte. I have to admit that all the stress, anxiety, and anger of that bankruptcy dominated our household. I could feel it. It was tough. I always knew that I didn't want that to be me, but it took years and years before I could create a different life for myself, one of financial abundance and security. It's so interesting because the late rapper Biggie Smalls said, "Mo Money, Mo Problems." You know, I always thought in my head, *Hey, those are the kinds of problems I would be down with.* But would I? The loss of our childhood home is a memory that remains today. When I travel back to Long Island I like to drive by it and just reminisce about all of the things that it represented for me.

The combination of the stress and sadness my parents felt contributed to my very unhealthy relationship with money. It was so bad that a few years ago, my husband had to open his own account because I wouldn't let him spend his own money. My dysfunctional relationship to money is part of the dirty south.

Let's break this down a bit. When I ask myself what money is, I am clear that it is a means to get what I need and it can contribute to having the things and experiences that bring me joy. It is *not* my happiness. This old theory that money is my happiness is what I want to believe is part of my dirty south. The reality is the world is full of money. There is money everywhere. We just need to embrace the fact that we deserve to have as much as we believe we want or need. Your dirty south is the belief that money is tied to your feelings and emotions. I mean, it can be if you let it, but it doesn't have to be. Money helps us get what we want but so does love, gratitude, hope, belief in our own ability, and many other elements.

In the story of my True North, money doesn't control me. It doesn't define me. I have a non-contentious relationship with it. We like each other, we do not depend on each other for emotional support. In the story of my True North, money is part of my daily gratitude. I end up thanking God and the universe for the money I have saved, for the blessings that will derive from it, and for its teaching in my life.

See, in the dirty south, money was never part of my gratitude story, so I now believe it never really showed up for me because I wasn't grateful for it. Yes, I could conjure up many reasons why money didn't show up for me—I wasn't a trust fund baby, my parents didn't save it for me, I was young and didn't understand its value so I spent it—but part of the realization of what my True North means to me is the understanding of money's place in my life. Yes, it has a rightful place but not a controlling place.

Keeping it all the way real, I still struggle with this sometimes, but the awareness of how I perceived money in the dirty south has contributed to the growth of how I look at it today. See, in the past, money was everything to me. I didn't understand how to manifest more of it. Today, I have grown. I see money as a small part of my life as opposed to it being my entire life. In my True North, money is good, it's helpful, I recognize it supports my survival, but it doesn't control my emotions, my happiness, or my drive. It is my friend. It helps and I am grateful for it.

Some of my memories from growing up left an imprint on my life that trigger some uneasy emotions, but let's just declare right now that I am making the choice to live in enlightenment. I am making the choice to focus on love, connection, positivity, and engaging relationships with different parts of my inner being like my heart, my mind, and my soul and connecting to that of others. This is part of the journey that I call heading to my True North. For me, that place of solitude represents light. It's my center of genius, it ignites my creativity and my inspiration, it's that place where I strive to be at my best each day. It's my happy place. It's the place where my ego gets checked at the door. So, while I will honor my dirty south, it is *not* what I want to focus on going forward. No looking back, unless it presents an opportunity to heal from some of the self-inflicted wounds. Like most humans, I have at times allowed ego and self-doubt to rule my thinking.

Even though I had some challenges with my childhood, it never stopped me from wanting a family. In fact, I believe that families teach you so much about yourself and the world. I cannot imagine life without my siblings. Each of them holds a special place in my heart for a different reason. Life would not be the same without them.

I always thought I wanted three children at some point in my life, two boys and a girl. I never went as far as to name them, but I always imagined they would be a part of my adult life. You know the saying "God works in mysterious ways?" Well, mysteriously, I have children now and it's the perfect setup, but they are not mine.

I'll explain what that means in a second, but part of my True North is all about self-discovery. It's also the knowing that it is okay for my thinking to grow and change, to evolve as I evolve. I do not need to be tied to the same thinking I had fifteen years ago or even yesterday. The creativity of my thoughts is expansive. It grows, it changes, it views things differently.

Back to my desire for children: I asked for children and God gave me children. About a dozen of them! Including nieces and nephews and my beautiful goddaughter and the list goes on. Growing up in a large household, I distinctly remember big holiday gatherings around the dining table and laughing and enjoying family time with my siblings. I remember family trips and Sunday afternoon trips to our extended families' homes after my mom got off work. I also dreamed that I would create those memories with my children.

But as the saying goes, "When we make plans, God laughs." A few years ago, Michael and I discussed bringing kids into our home. I would tease him, "We can't have kids because you would let them go out and play in traffic!" and he would tease me, "Well, your kids would be in straitjackets and need tons of therapy because you would be so strict and always yelling at them." You know, while they probably wouldn't be in straitjackets, I admit they would certainly be yelled at on the daily.

See, when I was growing up, my parents didn't mess around. My mom ran a very strict household with very strict rules. An occasional spanking here and there was not out of the norm. We knew what we had to do and did it when it was time to do it. We feared, but we loved; no ifs, ands, or buts about it. I actually respect that style of parenting. I know my parents' parenting style contributed to my respect for others, my detail orientation, and my lack of procrastination, so needless to say, I am all the way here for it.

If I had children of my own, who knows if my kids would've tried to call Child Protective Services on me? It would be just my luck that I would have that child who did that. Why do I say that? Well, let's just say, one time in my teenage years, my mom and I were in a disagreement. We were downstairs in the basement of my childhood home. For whatever reason, the house phone was downstairs with us as well. I proceeded to tell my mom that I would call the police on her if she hit me or persisted whatever behavior she was exhibiting at the time. My mom, God rest her soul, picked up the house phone, handed it to me, and said, "Go ahead and call them." I was shocked, but she had pushed me to the brink so in my head, I was like, "Okay, I'll show her." I proceeded to dial 911, but before I could get to the last digit she said, "And just so you know, if you hit that last 1, I'll make sure you're dead before they even get here to take me away." I gently placed the phone down, pushed her out of the way, and ran out the house, bare feet and all. I knew that the fact that I even made it to 9-1 was a death sentence in and of itself, forget what was going to happen to me for pushing her. I laugh about it now but think I would be *that* parent. Maybe God knew that too and He felt it best not to give me any of my own. The interesting part, though, is he still brought me children, just not in the conventional way.

Michael and I volunteered in the youth program at our spiritual home, Center for Spiritual Living in Fort Lauderdale. Even though we both knew we would be challenged by the other's parenting style, this was our last chance to decide if we wanted to have children—neither of us was getting any younger. After two months of volunteering, Michael was done and said, "This is not for me." (Funny, the children loved him.) On the other hand, I came to a different realization—I loved children more than I thought.

I learned that when children belong to someone else, I can be as patient as all heck with them and they do help fill a space in my heart that longed to be filled. But I would rather travel and have drinks on the beach while not paying for a sitter. Having my own children wasn't for me, either.

Back to how God works in mysterious ways. Before we could even tell the youth ministry that we no longer wanted to volunteer, the Youth Director stepped down. There was this tugging in my heart, *You could be the new youth leader. You would love it; the extra money and you would be surrounded by the love of children. This is for you.*

The other part of me said, *I do not want to commit to anything, my time is my own. I already have a full plate with work and my personal and social life.* As moments and days went by, the tugging got stronger and stronger. I couldn't deny it. I had a chat with our Senior Minister and very skeptically asked questions about the role. He was great about it and answered my questions, but he tells me today, he knew even then it was my job to do. So, for the last three years, I have been the Youth Director. Those children light up my life with their innocence, love, inquisitiveness, lack of judgment, and creativity. And the best part about all of this is I can have an impact on their lives, love them, and then hand them back to their rightful owners.

But you see, realizing your True North is a bit about knowing that life does give us what we ask for, although it may not look exactly the way we expected it to. I asked for kids and I received them. Not in the traditional way, but in the way life, the universe, and God intended me to have them. Do I sometimes wish I had some of my own? Sure, every once in a while. But the truth is, my heart is full.

This experience taught me more valuable lessons about my True North. Life doesn't always end up the way we envision it. What matters is how open we are to seeing the beauty of life unfold. I also learned that when we ask, we truly do receive. How we receive it and when we receive it is not always up to us, but we certainly do receive.

Onto a whole other part of me that we really haven't visited yet. As a young adult, I always had a strong work ethic. At fourteen, I was working for a cabinetmaker making custom furniture. Work is part of my DNA. I consider myself to be a hard worker. I put my all into everything I do when it comes to work. I have the most amazing job right now! Funny, it is my dream job for reasons I never imagined. Let's go back to my college years and I'll explain more about my "dream job."

Life at C. W. Post College was fun. I even pledged a fraternity and had a very active social life. I valued college because I paid my own tuition out of my own pocket. I never wanted to take out loans and be indebted to Fannie Mae for the rest of my life. I really wanted to go to college. It was part of my destiny.

I worked at Edwards Superfood store while I was in college. That was such an experience. Let's say I made some mistakes with that job I am not proud of today but I can look back at it, laugh, and see how much I learned about the value of work and how to value an employer. My life was school and schoolwork during the day, work at night and on the weekends, and social life and studying in between! It was very challenging at times, but it forced me to live the values of hard work and dedication.

I always thought I wanted to be an executive of a big company. But what were the values that I needed a job to instill in me? During my college years, I got a job at JPMorgan Chase and Co. working as a customer service representative in the call center. I was pretty good at it. After all, I love people and relationship-building is my thing.

Yes, I also learned the art of defusing upset customers, "I'm just going to put you on hold for five minutes until you calm down and stop acting crazy." I heard the funniest things from people. I also heard some derogatory things too, but mostly what I learned by answering phones was how to be humble. I learned that people often just want to be heard, so why not listen to them?

After I graduated from college, I was promoted to a full-time role as a Quality Assurance Manager and shortly thereafter to a Marketing Communications Manager. I could finally practice what I went to school for. What I learned quickly was that marketing was changing by the minute. I had to be adaptable, do my own research, and keep praying. Fortunately, it was all second nature to me.

I worked for businesses like General Electric and American Express and learned so much about how businesses operate and how to work in a bureaucracy. Some of it was fun, some of it really sucked, but I learned from it all. Over the course of my professional years, I worked for an event production company, a digital marketing agency, and other brands, but the job that taught me the most about resiliency was my Director of Marketing job at a hair extension company. It turned into the most traumatic, unruly, and dysfunctional place I ever worked at. Yes, I got the chance to travel to countries I had never seen before and I am grateful for that experience, but I would ask myself if it was all worth it.

My boss started off as an amazing guy but demeaned me and others in the workplace and, while I knew it was hurting my soul, I stayed until I didn't have to stay anymore. I was asked by my boss if I was bipolar on one occasion (which I am sure could be a Human

Resources disaster) but since he was best buddies with the head of Human Resources, there was nowhere for me to go but out the door. I've talked to some of my past co-workers and learned that their souls were bleeding too.

So why do we stay in situations that we know are not healthy for us? Probably because, like the discussion about religion earlier, when we are so used to one thing we become paralyzed, no matter what it does to us or our belief system.

After I left that job, I could breathe again. Shortly after, I started working at my current job as a Director of Marketing at a dental practice. Yes, it has its challenges, but it's my favorite job ever because they value me and my thoughts and my ideas and they make it known. Do you know what that does for your ego after working in a nightmare? I'm so grateful. Okay, so it's not just my ego, but being valued is a core belief of mine. When I feel valued, I give something my all. One could say that a big part of the story of my True North is value. Do my friends value me, does my family value me? If I do not feel a level of value something feels off to me. Can you see how the importance of feeling valued is a theme throughout my life?

As part of my True North, I am learning more about the true essence of value. I get to define it. I get to determine when someone is not valuing me or my time. I get to decide. No one can tell me I am bipolar again. Well, they can, but it just won't have the same impact on me. I know I can walk away because the value system I have created for me will not tolerate that. I create, define, and embody value. My terms! It's awesome!

The other lesson on value is about how I value others, myself, and all the things that surround me. As I get older, I want to live a life of value. What does that mean? For me it means, how can I love more deeply and more boldly? How can I give to others that might need support? How can I empower people to empower other people to change the world? How can I show love and appreciation daily for all that I am, all that I will be, all that I have, and all I will receive?

I have come to learn that when you value all the things you have in life, more of those things or the things you need and want will come back to you.

True North for me is staying in an attitude of gratitude for all I have in life and appreciating the small things as much as the large things, understanding what is valuable to me and knowing I do not have to live with what doesn't feel valuable. Now, I will be the first to say that I fall short at times, but there is a still, small voice in my mind that reminds me that waking up each day is valuable and it's so awesome that I get to choose what my life is going to be like. Even when the day stinks and that perfect job gets on your last nerves, how amazing is it to say, I *love* my job, I adore my bosses and feel like they treat me like family, and I am blessed to work with smart people who are passionate about helping others get the best care imaginable. I value my team. I have the best people that work for and with me and who are considerate of me as an individual and not just as a boss, peer, or coworker. That is what the perfect job looks like. Part of the formula with value is that you get back what you put in. I am proud to say that because I love working for the dental practice, I too give it my all. You will sometimes see me working at 5 a.m. or 9 p.m., because I am committed to doing whatever it takes to have it be a success. Because I value it, it values me.

So, you may wonder why—if I have the perfect job—I have started my own business at nights and on the weekends. There are a few reasons. I'll get into those in a second but first, let me tell you about my business. My business is called Content Redefined and I help entrepreneurs and reinventors craft a marketing and content strategy that connects with their right audience and influences them to buy. At this stage in the game, I think you might be able to tell that connection is important to me. I believe that in marketing and branding, connecting with your audience is critical to the success of your products. Look at a brand like Disney, which is a perfect example of connection. You are not a customer to them like every other business; you are a guest. You have a real-life connective and creative experience when you go to Disney or purchase their products. Everyone wants to go to Disney. Why is that? Because they market to people's emotions. They use the world of the imagination to create an art form that engages kids, parents, and all people through multiple experiences. They are a prime example of great marketing. Yes, they do traditional marketing, but they use tactics like strong customer service and other connective approaches brilliantly to engage with people directly. And that is what my company is founded on. It's redefining a client's content and strategies to reach emotions.

One reason I started this business is because I am a good writer (I am hoping at this point you agree) but I also want to apply what I know to empower people. When we empower people to empower more people, we make an imprint on the world. That's my why. This business is my creative outlet as well as a means to keep those ugly feelings about money in check.

I also know that deep down inside, I want to prove to myself and others that anyone can make it big. Entrepreneurship is not a world full of disappointment and failure. It doesn't have to be. It takes perseverance, resilience, tenacity, and *time*, but it can be done. I built my business for my parents, to prove you can try new things and still be happy in the process. Yup, that's True North for me. The idea that I can grow this business, I can be successful, and I can help other people in the process without losing my happiness. Guess what? I am loving it. I have had the honor of meeting so many new people and, through practicing gratitude every day and a little help from my partners who help me execute on some of our business objectives, I am moving at a manageable pace, meeting new clients and having fun. So, as you can see from both my full-time job and my business, work can be awesome. It's all about what you make of it! True North!

They often say you save the best for last, so the biggest part of my True North story is my love, my partner and other half; Michael. I feel so blessed to have finally met someone who allows me to just be me. Yelling, screaming, OCD, detail-oriented, particular me. I often say to myself, *If I had ever met someone like me, I would've run on Day 1.*

Michael is the best. Like any other couple, we have our challenges here and there, but 95 percent of the time we are loving the life we are building. Among many other things, Michael has taught me to enjoy life and see the beauty in every aspect. He has taught me the value of gratitude, patience, and peace. He is the most peaceful and humble person you will ever meet. God knew I needed him and sent him and I am forever grateful.

When it comes to us, my True North means understanding that we are both human, we are different but we can come together and love each other anyway. This might be hard to believe (unless you know me personally) but I have a pretty slick tongue. I will have a nasty response to give anyone at a moment's notice, but how great is it to really be loved and supported unconditionally? I am learning that our partners are mirrors of what we want to be or what we strive to be. I want to be peaceful, calm, and just go with the flow, but that doesn't come easy for me. I live vicariously through Michael as he teaches me how much better life is sometimes when we just relax. I had to go through the dirty south in terms of relationships with others and myself to find him, but I did, and it's been the best journey. I wouldn't change it for the world because in those steps, I learned so much.

That is what my True North really means. It is founded on acceptance. Acceptance for all things, people, places, and experiences. It is also founded on the idea that no matter what you were taught or what happened in your past, you can change the narrative. You have the ability to manifest and ask God for what you want and need. Sit back, relax, and let it be delivered right to you. Just don't be surprised if it looks different than you thought; it was intended to be just that way. My True North is me, unapologetically, flaws and all. I can be fully expressive and let my creativity flow, not letting the words and actions of others deter me from being the best version of me. My True North is the realization that my dirty south was the path that led to my True North. Whether it was perceived or reality, it formed who I am and will teach me more about what I will become. My True North will allow me to be whatever I want to be today and it will let me change that tomorrow if I so choose. My True North is enjoying this very moment, every moment. My True North is unconditional love for everyone around me, including myself. Just the way I am! Love is my True North!

Kirby Monestime is a connoisseur when it comes to building relationships, striking up conversation and bringing collaborative energy to any room. As a Marketing Coach and Specialist, he has developed a system that integrates conscious thought and the law of attraction into developing creative content and marketing strategy.

CEO and Founder of Content Redefined, Kirby helps entrepreneurs and reinventors overcome the stigma that marketing and content creation is overwhelming and complicated. He helps clients develop a powerful and robust marketing strategy that connects with their ideal audience and influences them to purchase. Through the use of affirmative statements, creative market positioning, conscious thinking, and ego abandonment, Kirby provides winning solutions for his clients across the country.

With over 20 years of expertise, Kirby has found himself employed by Fortune 500 companies such as JPMorgan Chase, American Express, and General Electric brainstorming, developing, and leading large-scale marketing initiatives. As a student of Science of Mind principles, Kirby gives back as a Youth Leader for children through a

South Florida spiritual center. When not inspiring children or creating awesome marketing for new and emerging brands, you can find Kirby exercising, biking, dining out, or spending quiet evenings at home with his partner, Michael.

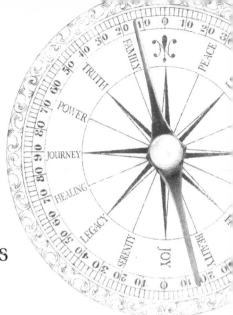

Lessons of Fireflies

Shara French

Dad taught me to shoot a gun with honor and respect.
Dad taught me to swim, ride a bike, and run fast.
He taught me to play pool.
He taught me to laugh.
He taught me to drink.
Dad taught me to be strong
and he taught me to love.

Lightning cracked and bounced off the bluffs while the thunder boomed across the Wisconsin summer sky at Gramma and Grandpa Van Dyck's house on Loomis Street in La Crosse, Wisconsin. Fairy tale summer vacations were spent there when I was a teenager. I remember my dad taught me how to catch a firefly in a mason jar. The magical, luminous green bugs appeared nightly at the steamy dusk. We sat on the concrete steps of their storm porch watching the shimmering green glow bugs hover just above the blue hosta bushes and red-berried juniper trees. We waited to softly catch one and gently place it in the jar. We would watch the bug's yellow-green glow pulse for hours and then let it go. Dad said you have to let the firefly go or it will die. Sometimes Mom called Dad "the dad." They are gone now. It makes me sad. I should have called them more during those years in the Marines. Lessons from regrets.

Dad was a Wisconsinite and a proud Packer fan. As a Westby High School senior he earned a football letter jacket. Dad's cherished jacket was made of maroon wool with white crinkly stiff leather sleeves. Jacket-proud Dad.

After high school, Dad joined the Marine Corps. What made him join? Dad's younger brother, Uncle Doug, said, "It was simple. Father told your dad that after high school, he was on his own; get a job or join the military." But why choose the Marines? I remember Dad telling me the Marines were the toughest branch of service. Maybe that was why. Dad was second oldest of his family. His sisters, except Barb, were younger than him. When he went home on leave they would surround him and hug him in his uniform. My aunts Barb, Linda, Kathy, and Sandy would gather around their brother at the kitchen table, enamored, listening to his colorful military adventures. They were so proud of him.

Dad kept a small silver-studded metal suitcase filled with all his precious Marine Corps things: hats, emblems, badges, canteen cups, John Wayne can openers for C rations, and pictures of him partying with Asian women in Japan. He took that suitcase everywhere he went, even desert camping, which we did nearly every summer for two weeks at the Salton Sea desert in Riverside.

The last desert trip before we moved to Montana was no different than any other; the suitcase came with us. We always had a blast target practicing with our .22 rifles and gold-mine hunting. Dad taught us important safety rules for handling guns. He strongly emphasized how important it was to always point a weapon away from your body and to never, ever point it at anyone else. "Do not point your weapon at anything you do not intend to shoot," he would say. He was very serious about firearm handling and constantly stressed safety. Dad showed us how to thoughtfully set up target practice by placing beer and coke cans strategically up and down the red dirt canyon slopes. "What we brought in, we take out," Dad said. That meant trash and ammo shells. The desert was pristine and beautiful and meant to stay that way. Dad was always the respectful teacher.

Scented purple sagebrush bushes dotted the landscape as we drove around the hot dusty desert searching for anything old and unique we could find. Old rusty railroad tracks that were still in service and abandoned gold mines were points of interest in our daily off-road excursions. One time we found an old tarnished fork, a brittle newspaper from 1936, a parched blonde-haired baby doll with its left eye popped out, and some shiny, rocky chunks of blue-green copper ore.

On the way back from one of those trips, Dad's silver suitcase flew out the side door of our camping trailer, but we didn't know it until we got home. He was so upset. When we drove up the driveway and parked after our long trip, the side door was still flopped open. A bag of my favorite shirts had flown out, too. After that, Dad was much more protective of his things, especially his letter jacket. My mind still sees it hanging in the downstairs hall closet of our Simi Valley house.

Our house on Brentwood Street in Simi Valley, California, was a four-bedroom modern two-story with a built-in garage. The house Mom and Dad bought was sold *as is,* complete with a swimming pool, an old-fashioned green jukebox that still played 45s, and a pristine pool table that sat majestically in the two-car garage. A gold plaque stamped in the rail showed the pool table's official credentials, a Brunswick 1922 Competition Edition, Pocket Billiard. Sweet and sharp. Its side rails were made of polished dark amber-brown oak. Shiny yellow-gold braided tassels hung down from each of its six pockets. Deep Kelly green felt covered the sturdy slate. The wide table legs were oak too, thick and curved. Sexy. After seeing this perfect pool table, Dad was sold.

He taught me how to play pool and we played a lot. I fell in love with billiards because of him. He was consistently very serious about respect for the game and following official eight-ball pool rules, always with sportsmanship-like conduct. "Don't lean on the sides," he reminded me. "It's rude to the other player."

From the inside out, the entire house and property screamed with character. The large backyard featured a built-in rectangular swimming pool, ten feet deep, with a love seat, a white diving board at the deep end, and wide steps at the shallow end.

From a distance the water looked silky smooth with deep aquamarine blues and green hues, spectacularly sparkling. In the mornings before school, I would look out the kitchen window across the patio awning, through the honeysuckle vines, and watch the steam rise from the water. It was a heated pool. Dad was proud of that. Sometimes after school I would sit on the side and dangle my feet in the warm water and think about things.

Dad had the most perfect dive—no splash, like in the Olympics. All the neighborhood kids wanted to come over to our house to swim during the summer. Random knocks on the front door led to swimming, running around barefoot on the blacktop, swimming, eating bologna, cheese, lettuce, and tomato sandwiches, playing pool, and more swimming. Our house was *the* hangout house. Mom and Dad worked hard every day to give us a good life.

Dad was a police officer with the Los Angeles Police Department. Our lives on Brentwood Street changed the day he pursued a guy who was on phencyclidine (PCP). Users of PCP, also known as angel dust, show extra-human strength combined with violent and aggressive behavior. The guy on PCP pulled Dad's arm through the wrought-iron fence so hard that he dislocated my dad's shoulder and severely injured his neck. After he spent two months on convalescent leave, the LAPD decided to make major cuts in the department. This meant that instead of two policemen per patrol car, one policeman per car was the new rule. Respect the game, respect the gun, respect people— all important ideas for a kid to learn, but things were changing in our world. For Dad, it was time to move out of California.

During Christmas break of my junior year in high school, Dad told me and Van, my brother, he bought land in Montana and was thinking about moving us up there the following summer. "What!?" we said. *The summer before my senior year? No!* I thought. "Look at it as an adventure," he said.

I remember thinking, *I can't believe this is happening,* but the decision was made—we moved that summer between my junior and senior year in high school. I never really believed we would ever leave Simi Valley.

Random Acts, Violence, Drunkenness

Oh, Susanna, won't you cry for me? Dad's with the LAPD. Our new house is 2336 Brentwood Street. Devonshire Division and a banjo on his knee. A mansion over the hill. San Fernando Valley. Pool table, swimming pool, two-story. A vegetable garden and room to grow.
Slap happy. Dizzle, dazzle, kid amazed! No more Catholic school! Yay! Real clothes to wear. No uniforms! No white shoe polish Sundays. A buncha white kids. White cord wood stacked. Floyd's the only black guy. Letter jacket! Football tar! Popular. Team running back and super cool. Mom and Dad's Halloween parties. Crazy! Liquor oozed like goo in our swimming pool. Grown-ups acting like nincompoops. Dad's cop friend, six-foot Wally, drunk diving; eleven forehead stitches later.
Flash forward, a sister is born. Add water, instant baby watcher. Desolation? Rebellion? Suddenly, we moved to a Montana peak. Isolation is now the test.

California girl transplanted to snow-shrouded mountains in the Pacific Northwest. Seven miles south of the Canadian border sat the logging town of Eureka, Montana, population fifteen hundred. Clear, icy memories. I can still see the grand snowy Canadian Rockies and the moon that hung like a giant glowing white orb pressed against the starlit black sky. Icicles formed in my nostrils when I walked down the slushy, muddy road to catch the school bus.

From Simi Valley High School senior class of 700 to Lincoln County High School senior class of 66. Huge teenage adjustment. The Montana senior experience included a visit of the military recruiters to the high school gymnasium. Looking at the different branches of service set up there to persuade kids to join, I considered my options. There was only one option: my dad was a Marine.

Dad was the first man to love me and love me unconditionally. He was always there for advice, a shoulder, and just to hear his voice. I trusted his word and his confident, measured reassurance that never failed me. He guided me to my early True North by teaching me to love and to respect myself and respect important things like guns and nature and people. I thought, *Since Dad was a Marine, I will join the Marines. That will get me back to California too.* Kid-brain thinking. In 1980 I boarded a plane for the first time, headed to Marine Corps boot camp, Parris Island, South Carolina. Insert chaos.

Desolation, Complication
in God's Country, Eureka!

Mouths fraught with random allegations. They were fumbled, fooled, and looped. Canadian Rockies in my backyard. High-waisted snow. Icicles in my nose. Real confederacy up north, far away from the Union Jack. Only white people here. A cop's kid is bad luck, struck and shunned. Senior year sucked. A non-hick in a new-hick town. Eureka Tavern and Café. A waitress...and good tips. Cop dad got Southern Comfort whiskey shots in his plastic coffee to-go cup for sips. Go to school, work, go to school, work. Our house was the chicken coop. Logger Days, bull riding, bed racing, and demolition derbies. May 1979. Recruiters Day in our school gymnasium. Thunderstruck, awestruck, dumbfounded, a Marine in a dress blue

uniform stood. Handsome. Clean cut. Fine. Maybe mine?
I raised my hand. Nineteen and flying. Parris Island.
Black and white lacy, frilly, prissy girl...to military con-
vert. Snap decision. No thinking. Smart salute. No restitu-
tion. Robotic. My life in chaotic orbit. Complete and utter
obliteration. Mental diversion, submersion into elaborate
deliberate coercion.

Six months later, standing on yellow footprints at Marine Corps
Recruit Depot, Parris Island, South Carolina, I am shaking uncontrol-
lably in the cold and getting yelled at. *What the hell did I get myself*
into? Finally, it is the end of the day. Lying in the top bunk at 7:30
p.m. on New Year's Eve 1980, I hear a girl screaming. She had a
plastic shaving razor and was trying to cut her wrists with it. She was
frantic! "GET ME THE FUCK OUT OF HERE! NOW! I DON'T
BELONG HERE. I WILL KILL MYSELF!" The Military Police were
called and she was removed from the squad bay in handcuffs. That's
the way they did it. I was nineteen and entering an aggressive, patriarchal military bastion where rules had serious consequences.

I had to adjust quickly to this alien environment or get handcuffed
and hauled off. I was a timid young woman, and I soon discovered it
was vital to act strong, to survive, to act like a man. As a Marine tyro
I quicky learned I had to integrate into the patriarchal environment of
the Marine Corps to survive and succeed.

Woman Marine (never forget it)
Firearm; copper-colored cartridge case. Pointy green-tipped
brass bullets. Glittering ammunition. Smooth cherrywood
butt stock and dove-gray painted gun metal. Big barreled
jeweled weapon. Marine's treasure. High-powered rifle
donned Marine. Machine gun, ammo-totin' mama. Peace,
protection, or propaganda? Symbols or honor? A woman
Marine. Remember it. Never forget it. You are a Marine
warrior goddess.

Appearance: be modest. Stay neat and attractive, always. A feminine hairstyle. Hair will not fall below the collar's lower edge. No adornment. Nails one-quarter-inch long from fingertip edge. No fancy foo-foo nail polish. Nix loop-de-loop fobs and baubles. Zero gaudy chokers or bangles. Limited jewels. One ring per hand, only. Tattoos okay. No gang affiliations. Bright red or purple lips forbidden. Think scantily clad, makeup applied generously.

Headgear; cover is a hat; hat top shaped like a stop sign. Eight razor-creased points atop. Decal ironed on is eagle, globe, and anchor emblem. Black emblem embedded, imprinted in your forehead like a brand. Crown hat or clown hat? Black Marine Corps emblem, symbolic, iconic, amniotic. Hypnotic. A brotherhood. Marine Corps' Hymn. Memorize all three verses. Forget? Black-ball punishment. Semper Fidelis, Latin for always faithful. Marine Corps motto.

A rigid twenty years in the Marine Corps brought me closer to my True North. Now, I cherish every free-minded moment reflecting on a past of twists and turns. During those twenty years, I traveled on orders to Japan, the Philippines, and the Middle East. For two of those years, I served as a Drill Instructor for female Marines. Drill Instructor duty was my most rewarding military experience and the most difficult mentally and physically. However, I did not initially choose this career path; it seems to have chosen me. I fit in well with the well-ordered repeated routines in training Marine Corps female recruits. They followed orders dutifully, pressing their uniforms and shining their boots like good little Marines, as I did. It was the strict structured environment that suited the instincts I developed in childhood from my dad that translated into effective recruit training leadership.

As the oldest of five children, I think I got the best of my mom and dad's love. I was the proverbial daddy's girl. They really gave me my "earth legs." But sometimes, life goes haywire—my parents divorced after thirty-six years of marriage.

I had sixteen years in the Marines when a phone call crushed my idea of the perfect family. My world shattered. My inner compass needle shot straight south. Mom was crying and saying Dad left her for someone younger. His humanness is judged. Should he be judged? I think not, now. But shock was a mild word in judgment I used then.

There are the good and the bad memories. Which ones to keep? Which ones are left behind, like dust? I will the painful memories to dust. The next day, I drove to Kingman, Arizona, for a virtual shit-show. Dad was running around the house with an overnight bag grabbing random things, tossing them in the bag, and muttering something like, "Shara... will...tell...your broth...leaving?"

"No. You tell him," I say.

He did, leaving my broken mom and my two teenage brothers behind. His teaching me right and wrong, his strong qualities of character in being a Marine and a police officer as examples, guided me in responding to that moment. But understanding his humanness and frailness took a decade to realize. I was still daddy's girl. The question was, *Why did he leave?* Driving back to the Marines on I-40 West, to a cushy La Costa apartment and a new husband, I kept thinking and asking, *Why did Dad do this? What is real?* Enter military distractions.

A Marine Corps career path proved rewarding as well as challenging. I often reflect on lessons learned when needing guidance today, especially those about being a woman in a man's world—the Marines. Traumatic experiences took place navigating this military world of patriarchs. However emotionally difficult these events were, I used them to help make future decisions with knowledge and discernment.

Reflecting on my career, I did my best to stay focused on my True North: to remain professional and respectful in all matters—relationships, nature, and myself. As a woman in the military, I mimicked aggressive male characteristics as an act of survival. The strict female Drill Instructors at boot camp taught me to be aggressive, using a loud voice. I was not purposely being deceitful; I used the action of aggressiveness to fit in with the male Marines, for survival and to avoid any perceived weaknesses in my character that would call attention to me.

Ten years later, Drill Instructor School was similar, but there was no female senior leadership. In Drill Instructor School, men occupied 95 percent of the leadership roles. Implied aggression was layered within every period of instruction by the men who taught the classes. Our class graduated 115 male Drill Instructors and 11 female Drill Instructors. As a Drill Instructor, I had to force myself to exaggerate my aggressiveness and toughness for effectiveness. Aggressive behavior is not my natural disposition. I felt like I was going against my grain. Surrounded by men in a military environment, was I acting falsely aggressive for survival? Yes, I was. Were there other women around me who I observed doing the same thing, assimilating to survive? Yes, I think there were. Will they admit this? That is the question of the century. Some will, and some will not.

I often felt I had to portray a split identity. Drill Instructor duty started halfway through my twenty-year career. As a Drill Instructor, yelling had to become second nature. There is a purpose for yelling at recruits: large numbers of Marines must respond immediately to orders. A principle of a Marine's ethos is quick reaction to orders, which is especially necessary in battle. One sign of a successful Drill Instructor was voice projection, getting the recruits to act quickly. Loudness and yelling are characteristics of aggressiveness, assertiveness, and leadership in this role and imply the qualities of a Marine. My natural disposition was, and still is, opposite to yelling and dominating others. Loud and assertive language and using dominating manners while training the recruits in my charge was a serious challenge. Emotionally spent, I managed to successfully complete two years of Drill Instructor duty at Parris Island, South Carolina, returning to Camp Pendleton in 1991. The duty of being a Drill Instructor, training, and caring for America's daughters, became the ultimate responsibility for me. This experience continues to be a strong influence on my life.

While unspoken, it was expected that I would be a leader of men and women. At the same time, it was implied that I should follow behind the men. When I checked into my first duty station, I was immediately asked if I could type. I was assigned as the company clerk, filing papers, making coffee for the office, and running mail call. I remained in this assignment for two years. From wearing the same uniforms as the men to hiking with fifty-pound packs up and down hills, I was expected to perform the same as the men, yet I was not treated equally. Outside appearances, like "acting" to fit in, and to be "one of the guys," were part of everyday life for female Marines.

Intuitively, I knew I didn't fit in. I experienced sexist and unequal treatment in the military. And I know fellow female Marines had the same experiences. Some still suffer from unequal treatment malaise from harassment, whether the incident was reported or not. No matter the laws or protections put in place by leadership to protect those who reported sexual harassment, those work environments remained silently hostile. Military women feared backlash if they reported sexual harassment, so often they would not report. When I reported an incident of sexual harassment, I was considered a whiner, weak, and a troublemaker. Fellow Marines judged me as the cause of the situation without knowledge of what happened. Because of gender, I was judged and shunned after I reported an incident that would challenge my idea of True North.

During my second overseas tour to Okinawa in 1994, I was assigned to a company of approximately 400 Marines, seven of which were women. At a company party one Marine who outranked me began chasing me around with his hands out as if trying to catch me.

I initially characterized this incident as innocent, but it soon turned invasive. This Marine's charging around at me continued despite the word "Stop!" When he pursued me in a weird manic way, I maneuvered away and continued to tell him to stop. Several times during the party, he reached his arms out with hands trying to grab me, again chasing me like a kid on a playground. I dodged his hands as he reached out at me in and out of groups of talking people. His actions became harassing. I repeatedly told him to stop. People were watching and thought it was funny. Unsettled by this incident, I left the party.

The next day, the Master Sergeant called me into his office. He told me I was being punished for some minor infraction of my duties. Intuition engaged; my True North was in question. I remembered this Marine chasing me the day before. Yesterday's event and today's reprimand did not make sense to me. This was becoming an improper situation, bordering on harassment. I got up to leave. He yelled at me, "SIT DOWN, GUNNY!" I sat down. I feared the reprisal from the other Marines if I reported him. I would be called a troublemaker. A senior Marine chasing me around the company party would be my fault. I would be accused. I remained quiet in my chair while he ranted about how screwed up I was. Finally, I left his office. After contemplating the repercussions, I decided to officially report his harassing behavior. Almost immediately, I was called into the Company Commander's office. He was extremely upset. The whole situation became my fault.

Because I officially reported harassment, I became the target. The senior leadership (mostly men) in my company found out about me reporting harassment charges. False accusations of my misconduct began circulating around the company, an attempt at retaliation for reporting a harassment complaint. Then the Company Commander began accusing *me* of the harassing conduct. Nothing official was filed against me regarding misconduct because there was nothing to report. I did not trust anyone around me.

Shortly after this incident, I was reassigned to another unit for "safety reasons." Reporting this injustice eventually served as protection for the other women who remained in my former unit. My hope was that the men holding senior leadership positions there would think twice before mistreating one of those other woman Marines. Writing about this incident exposes the inner workings of some military units related to gender conflict. This is a true story about the underrepresented military women's community. There are many more stories like this. The Colonel who reassigned me after this incident gave me some wise advice. He said, "Gunny, if you stay professional in all your interactions with your fellow Marines, you can never go wrong." Wise words that do not fail me, ever. Another important example of moral courage and dedication to principles is modeled by my mom as I again reflect on my childhood memories.

Mom's baby sister, Joy, died when I was eight. Aunt Joy favored me over my brother, Van. I was her favorite. She would give me a popsicle and hide me behind the bedroom door to eat it, fast, before Van could see. We'd listen to Janis Joplin's *Big Brother and the Holding Company* album together on Dad's reel-to-reel. I loved her and I miss her. Chaos starts.

Gone at nineteen. Aunt Joy was on barbiturates and drinking wine while driving on the Pomona freeway. On a curved off-ramp she crashed into a light pole. Her husband had left her, jumping on a train with another girl. Couldn't take the leaving, the sadness, her heart ripped out. Her coma lasted four days. Grandma's horrible howls are imprinted, forever. Dad's cop connections got my Uncle Mike out of juvenile hall for her funeral. Uncle Mike broke his sister's fingers into a peace sign across her chest at the viewing while she lay in her white satin tufted casket. Dad almost broke his face. A death truth.

Mom's empathy and love for me is seared in my heart. I did not go to her viewing and Mom did not force me. I think she knew it would hurt me to see Aunt Joy lying dead in a casket. I thank my mom for not forcing me to go to the viewing. At the cemetery I wear a yellow and white zip-up dress and hold a purple rose, watching as her beautiful wooden casket is lowered into the earth. An unmarked grave is her resting place in Los Angeles. Sadness.

After fifteen years in the Marines, I began to see myself differently. I realize that I am carving a way to my True North into deeper meanings of honor and respect for myself and other people. I am grateful for this Colonel's sage advice and proud to serve our country as a United States Marine. I think back to when I joined the Marines. Mom cried when the recruiter came to our house in Montana. But she and Dad signed me in when I was seventeen. It was hard for her. Mom was the epitome of courage, loyalty, and dedication. She was courageous to let me go. She was loyal to my dad and dedicated to her family. She taught me the True North of the heart. I got the best of both my mom and dad. They gave me a strong, faithful, and loving foundation to live my best life. Thank you, Mom and Dad, for loving me. Unconditionally.

Beginning
Growing Meaning, Like Bean Seeds

Unbelievable notions are risqué rubbing protons. Unlike goddesses when they stalk, they crest like a wave. A peacock. I hated Baywatch. Unfondled covers stretch for days. Mother's hair was always coiffed in beehives. Norwalk. Fragmented filaments practice all kinds of archaic rudiment. Rudipoot. Crackled, cackle coconut. Who's the crackhead? Skid row. Paddy wagon. Double-handled baton. Dirty dungeon and a Dixie down. Shelter and sweetness. Happy.

A baby plays, crawling over a crack in the sidewalk on an effortless day...Mom hanging freshly washed sheets through backyard summer rays. Warm breezes a sweet honeysuckle scent. A clothesline tight rope. Summer.

We grow bean seeds in cotton cups every day. A habit is a habit is a habit. Mother Teresas they are not. Tight white faces stretched and pulled back wearing their fierce black and white cone-shaped hats. Dark coffee bean eyes, with sweet, dimpled pastry cheeks.

A hummingbird flits. I see the sun. Ruby red neck reflects. Shimmer neck back and forth, back, and forth, red-green-red, reflects, reflects, reflects. Santa Fe Springs. Railroad track city by a Catholic church. Saint Pious X Catholic School. Second grade. My First Holy Communion. A little girl in a communion dress slapped a priest. Not me. I saw it. I know it. I never forgot it. 1970. Aunt Joy died.

California native Shara French was recruited into the Marine Corps at the age of seventeen after moving to Montana. Shara proudly served her country for twenty years as a trained Ammunition Technician and retired as a Gunnery Sergeant in 2001. In 1994, Shara deployed to Kuwait for the national training operation Native Fury. Her most rewarding duty was the coveted position of Drill Instructor for women recruits at Parris Island, South Carolina. During her last two years in the Marines, Shara served as Leadership Coordinator for her unit, where she organized and facilitated leadership workshops while teaching Steven Covey's *The Seven Habits of Highly Effective People* to both active-duty military and civilian personnel.

Since retirement, Shara has followed her dream of higher education, culminating in a Master of Arts in Literature in 2017 from California State University–San Marcos with an emphasis on Creative Writing.

For Shara, writing is experimental; she manipulates language, content, and form to create new ways of hybrid writing while focusing on themes of personal narrative, short story, and poetry, and how those genres creatively intersect. Her published work includes *Worlds Apart: An Evolving Woman, One Female Marine's Assimilation into Patriarchal Spaces, and the Grief Coda* (Master's Thesis); *Growing Meaning Like Bean Seeds*; and *Molly Ann* (University Chapbooks). Other recent works include the poem *Woman Marine, (never forget it)* and short story *The Death Knock*, published in the Veterans Writing Group collaborative book *Listen Up! Things I Learned in the Military* and *Stories That Must Be Told* respectively.

Shara is a lifetime member of the Veterans of Foreign Wars and Auxiliary, attending monthly meetings as a trustee with a focus on the active-duty and retired military communities. Past volunteer work included hosting meetings for the North County Veterans Writing Group. Her current projects are shaping and honing her memoir, learning all she can about indie publishing, and spending time tending to her fairy garden. Her life revolves around a loving husband, her writing, and a precious cat colony.

Journey of Discovery

Susie Brown

This week, I stopped at our community pool for a swim. When I parked, directly in my line of sight was a pink and red golf cart with a license plate that read ABUELITA framed by a license plate holder that proclaimed *Life is Short—Live It!*

I became an *abuelita*—literally "little grandmother" in Spanish— thirteen years ago. When I first met my granddaughter, Emma, she was four months old and I had just survived Stage 4 throat cancer. During the long months of chemo and radiation, my mantra was, "I am going to live to see my granddaughter." Definitely, the odds were against me, so the words *life is short* took on a meaning that cut to the core of my being.

My heart, soul, and spirit, who I was, and all of my life up to that point came into clear focus. What was my True North? What were the guiding principles and values that would strengthen and sustain me in the face of this challenge? The totality of my life experience—all of my relationships, education, careers, adventures, and passions— was hanging in the balance. On one side, my past, and on the other side, all my hopes and dreams for my future.

With the help of God, skillful doctors and technicians, prayers of Christian and Buddhist friends, and the constant, loving support of my family, I made it. By some wonderful miracle, some fantastic twist of fate, the outcome was *Live It!* And with a profound sense of gratitude, I have.

The essence of my life and journey began long ago and very far away in the lands of Scotland, Germany, Ireland, and Bohemia. The year was 1676, one hundred years before the Declaration of Independence, when two Dodds brothers sailed from Scotland to America. They were in the employ of a wealthy Scotsman and would work for seven years on his land in South Carolina in exchange for their passage. Their future held generations of the Dodds family who moved from South Carolina to Kentucky, north to Illinois and Iowa, and westward to Utah and California.

In the 1800s, a German couple with the last name of Werner, sailed from the port of Danzig across that same Atlantic. Their journey was motivated by the dream of religious freedom, which they realized in their new home of Illinois. The descendants of the Dodds and Werners met in California and that is where my dad, William Dodds Werner, was born.

Eighty years later, Denis and Susan Kelliher left Ireland in the wake of the potato famine. Their passage to America took them to New Orleans, and then up the mighty Mississippi River to Chicago. Once there, they secured jobs with the Marshall Field family, owners of one of Chicago's finest department stores. Their son, John James Kelliher, grew up to become a postmaster and married Christine Kralovec (they were my grandparents and their daughter Marion Christine Kelliher was my mother).

Like the Kellihers, the Kralovec family immigrated to America in the 1880s. They had come from a town near Prague, in what was then known as Bohemia. Bohemia was later renamed Czechoslovakia and then divided into the Czech Republic and Slovakia. The Kralovec family started with a farm near Green Bay, Wisconsin and had eight children. Later, they opened a general store in the small dairy farming community of Rosecrans. The only other business for miles was a cheese factory on the other side of the road. The second story of my great-grandparents' general store was a large dancehall, my mother's favorite place to visit on summer holiday. When it was empty during the weekdays, she would dance for hours around the large wooden floor, practicing the polka. On Saturday nights the dancehall would be filled with the local farmers and their families, singing, "Roll out the barrel, we'll have a barrel of fun."

Flash forward to the year 1950 at the Hollywood Palladium; Big Band music is blaring with trumpets and the tom-tom beat of the drums. The dance floor is filled with couples doing the Jitterbug, Lindy, and West Coast Swing. One couple is smiling and laughing as they share their first dance together. He is so handsome with sparkling blue eyes—and what a great dancer! She is a brown-eyed beauty who really knows how to twirl and swing—and what a sense of humor!

Bill was an airplane mechanic who had been stationed in Fairbanks, Alaska during World War II. Marion was born in Chicago and came out west to Hollywood after the war and became a teller at the Bank of America. During their courtship, they drove up to Ventura where Marion watched Bill race a midget car he had built himself. They also sailed to Avalon on Catalina Island. This adventurous couple married in December of 1950 and, by the following October, Susan Marie Werner (that's me) was born.

I have always felt that to know where I was going in life, it was vital to know where I had come from. Family history and genealogy is one of my passions. As I reflect upon the brave journeys my ancestors made to create a new future in a new land, I feel overwhelmed with gratitude for their determination and perseverance. Some made the journey seeking freedom to practice the religion they held dear. Others came in hope of rich farmlands. Those fleeing the horrendous potato famine in Ireland were driven by starvation and sheer survival. Perhaps those two young Scots were seeking the adventure of discovering a whole new world and the North Star helped to guide them to their future home, a future filled with a line of descendants that includes me. Each carried within them a code with qualities of strength and fortitude, a secret code passed from generation to generation. That code is within me. I have passed it to my children and they in turn have passed it to their children.

Going to visit Nana, my dad's mother, was a trip to the land of creativity and imagination. She was the family historian and a wonderful storyteller. Nana lived in a small white cottage in Culver City which she named the Tuckaway. Her lot was narrow but as long as a football field. The huge front yard led up to a fishpond with polliwogs, goldfish, and lily pads.

After I climbed up the brick stairway to her front door, the first thing I saw was her grand piano. It dominated her small living room; this was where she gave piano lessons. Next to the piano was a large woven basket full of percussion instruments—a tambourine, maracas, claves, castanets, a guiro, and finger cymbals. She also had a drum that she made from a small redwood planter barrel topped with a cowhide. My favorite instrument was her autoharp. To make a chord, I just had to press one of the buttons, hold it down tight, and strum while I made up my own songs. Sometimes, Nana would put a record on the record player and I would dance in the light and warmth of the fireplace. It felt magical.

Behind the house was her patio next to an enormous rubber tree. Up a little hill in the far corner of the backyard was her ceramic studio. She loved working with clay and signed her work Felicity, her artist's name. The ceramic studio really was her happy place. I was only four years old when Nana gave me my first lesson on throwing a pot. She had a standing potter's wheel and upended an orange crate for me to stand on. With her arms around me, she gave a kick to the bottom wheel and the top wheel spun around. We took a ball of clay and threw it into the center of the spinning wheel. We wet our hands with water, stuck our thumbs in the middle of the ball, pushed down to make the base, and pulled upward on the sides with our fingers. Wow, that lump of clay was transformed into my very first pot. As soon as the pot was dry, she would put it in her kiln for the bisque firing. Then, on my next visit, I would be able to paint on the glaze before the second firing. I could hardly wait to go back.

Bedtime was story time at Nana's. She had a beautiful polished wood rocking chair with plenty of room for two. While I snuggled up nice and cozy on her generous lap, she would read to me from *One Thousand and One Nights*. The tales of Scheherazade, a master storyteller of the ancient East, were filled with mystery and adventure, including those of Sinbad the Sailor battling monsters at sea and Aladdin flying through the skies on his magic carpet. These powerful stories helped to fuel and form my imagination.

After we hopped into bed, the stories would continue with the true tale of Nana's grandfather, a wagon master who led five expeditions of pioneers in covered wagons from Missouri to Salt Lake City on the Overland Trail. On one of these expeditions, Nana's grandfather was bringing his pregnant wife to their new home in Salt Lake City. Before they could reach their destination, she went into labor and gave birth to their daughter, Armina, in the wagon. Not long after, their wagon train was encountered by a band of Native Americans in Utah Territory. They approached the wagon where baby Armina was held in her mother's arms. "What happened next, Nana?" I asked anxiously. She replied, "Well, they took her and held her for a long, long time, looking into her eyes, and then they handed her back to her mother.

And when Armina became a woman, she married my dad and became my mother." Reflecting on this story years later, I ask myself, *What did they see in Armina's eyes? What would have happened had they taken her away to their village, perhaps to comfort one of their wives who had lost her baby in childbirth?* If Armina's journey had taken a different path, my Nana would not have been born, her son (my dad) would never have been born, and I would not even exist. It amazes me to think how one choice, one moment in time could have changed everything.

Today, Nana's percussion instruments (along with many more I have collected in my travels) are in a basket in my living room. It has been a joy to share them at drum circles, around a bonfire at the beach, and in classrooms with enthusiastic preschool children. I'm co-leader of the Rhythm of Life Drum Circle here in Laguna Woods, and Nana's and my instruments have been played by happy senior friends and neighbors for over a decade. Of course, they are a favorite attraction when my grandchildren come to visit at their Nana's house.

The love of music and dance is an important hallmark of our family life. Dance, dance, dance—that was the driving passion of my teen years. I grew up watching American Bandstand on TV and practicing all the latest dances like the Twist in my living room. At the junior high sock hop we danced the Jerk and the Mashed Potato. My friend Nick and I won a twelve-hour dance marathon at the West Covina teen center—we were really dancing in the zone that day! Soon, we found other popular places to dance in Southern California. Wednesday nights, Sorensen Park in Whittier featured great local bands and lots of room to do the Stroll. Fridays, the Rendezvous Ballroom on Balboa Beach was the place to do the Surfer Stomp with Dick Dale and his Del-Tones. The wooden dance floor would be bouncing as hundreds of teenagers released a massive wave of energy, all stomping on the same beat. Saturday nights, we cruised Sunset Boulevard in

Hollywood in the back of an El Camino, stopping to dance at Gazzari's or Whisky a Go Go. Our favorite dances then were the Hitch Hike, the Pony, and the Swim. The Shrine Auditorium was one huge dance floor that extended right up to the stage. That is where I saw a nineteen-year-old Rod Stewart sing with Jeff Beck. What I liked best about the concerts there was that it was not a sit-down venue for spectators; there was plenty of room to move and get creative with the live electric sounds.

I shifted gears from rock-and-roll to folk dancing in my twenties. Cal Tech in Pasadena offered international folk-dance classes. There, I learned from those who had memorized the steps and patterns of traditional dances from all around the world. I wondered later if the repeating patterns held a special appeal to the scientists and mathematicians in the group. A Greek taverna in Los Angeles was a friendly community gathering place where they taught and passed on the ancient dances that tied them to memories of their homeland—*Just follow the guy waving the big white handkerchief.* In the Fairfax District of Los Angeles, Israeli dance lessons required athletic prowess with lots of running and jumping. Note to self: *Next time, bring a dry change of clothes.*

Appalachian clog dancing and square dancing came next with the added perk of dresses with huge petticoats and tap shoes. While in college in Chico, California I joined the Folk-Dance Club and made lifelong friends. We still dance together at summer reunions at California WorldFest in Grass Valley, California. My path was leading ever northward from Southern California to Northern California and on to the northwest of Washington State. I was searching for new challenges and new adventures.

In Seattle, I fell in love with contra dancing. Weekly classes and dances were held in Ballard, North Seattle. This dance style has origins in Scottish country dancing and somehow, it felt so natural and easy to learn the steps. Maybe the music activated my secret code of Scottish DNA.

A marathon of events, the four-day Northwest Folklife Festival (the festival will be celebrating its fiftieth anniversary virtually in 2021), was held in Seattle Center on Memorial Day weekend, offering dancing all day and night. The next event was a fiddler's festival in Port Townsend just a ferry ride across the Puget Sound from Seattle. A week-long camp culminated in a fantastic performance by the students of all ages and a contra dance party which lasted all night long. Dancing until the first rays of dawn was something I had long dreamed to do; it was exhausting and exhilarating. Seattle also offered another four-day music event on Labor Day weekend called Bumbershoot with every genre of music and another opportunity to wear out those dance shoes. I spent five years working and living in the Seattle area with opportunities for family camping and skiing trips. Those trips were wonderful, but the experiences of dancing there are the ones that made the most profound and lasting impression on my spirit.

A family emergency brought us back to Southern California for a short stay to care for my aunt and our stay extended into years. My journey north had taken a big U-turn, but my inner compass told me I was right where I needed to be helping my dear aunt. During this time, I took Hula lessons from a dancer who had performed with Don Ho in Hawaii, so of course we learned the dance for "Tiny Bubbles." Before taking a trip to the Dominican Republic I took lessons in their native dance, the Merengue. I had done my homework and when on a snorkeling excursion we had a Merengue break, the captain yelled, "Somebody drive this boat, I'm gonna dance with this woman."

Another form of dance and one that is very liberating is Trance dance. It is a free-form dance with no partner required; you just move to the music in your own interpretive way. I found a place called Let's Dance in Seattle's University District and one in downtown Santa Monica, as well as a midnight trance dance party in Grass Valley and another at the Bellas Artes school in San Miguel de Allende, Mexico. In fact, at the dance in Mexico I met two women from San Francisco who had also attended the Grass Valley dances.

In my community of Laguna Woods, I have danced with the Folk-Dance Club and the Square Dance Club and attend social dances with Line Dancing. Our Hula group danced for the 90s Club; yes, we have lots of active ninety-year-old residents here. Maybe it's all the dancing that increases longevity. I finally made it to Woodstock via our annual Baby Boomer summer event, with lots of rock-and-roll and so many tie-dyed shirts we needed shades. I guess I have come full circle to where I started.

Music and moving with the music brings me abundant joy. This creative self-expression releases endorphins which make me feel energized and happy. When the vibrations are pulsing through my body, I feel ecstatically alive.

One of the things I missed most in 2020 was dancing with my friends and neighbors at our TGIF and Baby Boomer dance parties. I am looking forward to the day we can all laugh and let loose on the dance floor together again.

As I danced through my life, I came upon an important and powerful tool—creative visualization. "The journey of a thousand miles begins with a single step" was written on the bottom of a poster showing a sunlit path through a lush green forest. The poster was on the wall above my kitchen sink and I hung curtains and a valance around it to form a window, a window to my future. I was a single mom with two young daughters and had just begun science classes at Shasta College in Redding, California. My goal was to become a nurse and it would take several years to reach that goal. Every day as I washed my dishes, I would look at that poster and think, "If I just stay on this path and keep moving forward, I am going to make it." I enjoyed returning to college as a motivated adult student and within two years I had graduated with my Associate of Science degree. I then transferred to California State University–Chico where I earned my Bachelor of Science in Nursing, graduating with honors. As a speaker for our class commencement, I addressed the theme, "Making a Difference." I had found that having a positive mindset and visualizing completing my goal had been essential to my success. My poster had made all the difference in achieving my goal.

A few years later, after working as a charge nurse at the local hospital in Chico, I was feeling the urge to move on, the need for change. At a friend's apartment I saw another poster, one of Seattle with Mt. Rainier in pink alpenglow. It was so spectacular, I gazed at that poster for the longest time and then said, "If we look at this picture long enough, we can just jump into it and be there." And that's what happened: within a year both my friend and I had moved to Seattle. We had graduated together in nursing school and independently we found jobs and apartments in the Seattle area. Once again, I believe the power of visualization played a part in this major shift in my life. I had traveled to the great northwest in search of my True North.

New Mexico, the Land of Enchantment, was the place I chose to celebrate making it to my fifty-sixth birthday, the first year of my new post-cancer life. Albuquerque is home to the International Balloon Fiesta, which was the main event of this autumn adventure. I also wanted to follow the trail of the extraordinary artist Georgia O'Keeffe to Santa Fe and Taos and a tour of her home in Abiquiú was also on my itinerary.

After landing at Albuquerque (ABQ) on a bright, sunny October morning, my first stop was the Albuquerque Museum. The main exhibition room was filled with the largest collection of Native American art I'd ever seen. Standing in the middle of the room was a life-size horse draped in gorgeous, intricate seed bead work from head to tail. Silver and turquoise needlepoint jewelry, woven baskets and rugs with geometric patterns, and ceramic vessels were all exquisite examples of the many different styles of art found in the individual native nations from all parts of the United States and Canada. A prominent Navajo doctor and his life's passion for collecting these superb examples of artistry led to the preservation of true treasures.

Lunch with sharks? Sharks in the middle of the desert? Yes, a visit to the ABQ BioPark Botanic Garden was my destination for the day. In the dining room, the entire glass wall looks into a tropical underwater world and outside are beautiful gardens for an afternoon stroll.

I was ready for the drive north to Santa Fe where my first stop was the local Trader Joe's. I had been working at the Laguna Hills Trader Joe's for eight years and made a point to visit our other stores wherever I traveled. I shopped for water and snacks and told the friendly cashier I was a crew member from store #39. She asked why I was visiting Santa Fe and I replied, "I'm celebrating my birthday." As I walked to the car, she came running across the parking lot with a bouquet of flowers saying, "Happy Birthday!" What a great welcome! This was going to be a wonderful trip.

I spent the entire next day exploring the Museum of International Folk Art. A representation of the whole world was laid out before me in miniature and I was a giantess, like Gulliver, carefully walking around the tiny towns and villages and seeing the homes and people from all around the globe in colorful detail.

First Thursday nights in Santa Fe are Art Walk Night with many of the museums offering free admission, including the Georgia O'Keeffe Museum. Fabulous art galleries surround the main plaza where a rock-and-roll band was playing, people were dancing, and a classic car show was in progress. I walked into a shop and tried on knitted fur hats, maybe the blue one or the green one? Yes, the pink one is my birthday present! Every time I wear that hat I'm reminded of that wonderful night in Santa Fe. Ready to head back to my hotel I followed the sounds of jazz into a nearby bistro for tapas and wine and a few moments to think of the serendipity of spontaneous surprises that were finding me on this trip.

The morning's drive took me north past groves of golden aspens to Chimayo. El Santuario de Chimayo is a miracle site where some believe the soil holds healing power. Shrines have been erected by the recipients of these healings or by grateful family members. I made a small woven cross of grass entwined with flowers as my offering of gratitude for the miracle of my life and my healing from cancer.

By evening I had reached Taos, just in time to enjoy their monthly Art Walk and a film festival. What a terrific way to get to know a new place! I almost broke into song, "these are a few of my favorite things." Saturday morning, I strolled through the city park surrounded by colors of every shade and hue—the Wool Festival was in town. Booths were set up like a country fair and spinners sat happily at their wheels turning fluffy wool into yarn. They even let me give it a try. As one who loves to knit, crochet, and weave, I had hit the mother lode. I came away with brilliant lush yarn for future projects and a sense of belonging to this community of the Wool Women. Later that day, I drove outside town to the Taos Pueblo and walked through the thousand-year-old adobe village with a local guide who shared the history of this amazing place.

The next day I was walking through Georgia O'Keeffe's home in Abiquiú on a very different guided tour. What struck me as odd was how stark and plain it was—and her tables were made of sawhorses and planks of wood. What an unexpected contrast to her elegant and colorful floral paintings. From there I headed north to the Ghost Ranch where Georgia had painted many dramatic landscapes. I had brought my watercolors and found the perfect shady spot with a view of the inspiring red, rust, and ochre mountains and began to paint.

Outside Taos in nearby Arroyo Seco, I stayed for two nights at the SnowMansion Taos Adventure Lodge and Hostel. The highlight was a dance party in the main room around the circular ski lodge fireplace. Early the next morning I began the eighty-four-mile journey on the Enchanted Circle Scenic Byway, including stops to see the grave of D. H. Lawrence and the Vietnam Veterans Memorial in Angel Fire. The highway climbed through the mountains above 8,000 feet to Red River and Eagle Nest before descending into Taos. Continuing on the day's journey I stopped to see the Rio Grande River, then headed in the direction of the hot springs.

Going to the Our Greater World Earthship Community happened by chance after seeing the strange, futuristic homes on the mesa. I was amazed to visit a model Earthship made of earth-packed tires and other recycled materials like bottles and cans, designed to be sustainable with solar and some wind power.

After a long day of driving, Ojo Caliente was the perfect spot for dinner and a relaxing soak in the hot mineral waters under the night sky. Driving back that night, I pulled off the highway, away from the lights of the town, and got out of the car. I stood facing north and gazed up at the full expanse of the clear, star-filled desert sky. I felt my spirit reach upward, open, and connect with the greatness of the Universe. A river of overwhelming gratitude flowed through me with a total sense of peace, a knowing I was on the path of my True North.

Heading back to Albuquerque for the last day of this wonderful adventure, I encountered the Dawn Patrol at the Balloon Fiesta. In the early-morning darkness, the Dawn Patrol is the first small group of hot air balloons to ascend and test the box winds. Already, hundreds of spectators had arrived to find the balloons laid out carefully in long straight rows on the ground and they watched as the first row inflated their balloons with great blasts of flames and ascended. The balloons looked like giant floating light bulbs. Then the second row floated up to catch the wind. Row after row after row soared upward until the sky was filled with hot air balloons of every color and shape. Hey, there goes a cow, a stagecoach, an astronaut! Two bumblebee balloons ascended as one, locked in a kiss, then bid farewell as they floated apart. A beer stein all the way from Germany and a giant four-leaf clover reminded me of my mom and dad who loved to travel to this festival in their retirement. I had seen lots of photos of the event but this was my first time to experience it, and it was awesome.

It was time to bid farewell to the Land of Enchantment for now with hopes to return. Before leaving for New Mexico my only plan had been to see the Albuquerque Balloon Fiesta and Georgia O'Keeffe's home in Abiquiú. What I received was a giant birthday cake from the Universe inscribed with the words, *To Susie with Love. Here Are All of Your Favorite Things. Enjoy!* My trip was certainly a hundred times better than I had planned or imagined.

In conclusion I would like to share about one of the most influential teachers I have encountered on my path to find and follow my True North, Joseph Campbell. Reading his books and watching his lecture series on the universal themes in mythology from cultures around the world resonated deeply within my own spirit. They inspired me to form a philosophy of life and to follow my spiritual path in a much larger context, a path that allowed me to see my fellow travelers with more understanding and compassion. Campbell said, "If you follow your bliss you put yourself on a kind of track that has been there all the while, waiting for you, and the life that you ought to be living is the one you are living."

When I follow my bliss, I recognize and honor my essential true being and the values precious to me. I find my True North and follow it in the direction that leads to fulfillment and an unshakable state of peace.

In searching for the words to express my life experiences relating to my True North in this chapter, I began by making a list of my top ten values: Gratitude, Kindness, Love, Family, Community, Joy, Generosity, Humor, Adventure, and Passion. Those who I love and admire modeled these attributes. They were leading by example and I wanted to follow and emulate these qualities and values.

Moving forward on my journey, I have chosen love and kindness to be my guides in my relationships and interactions with others. There were times when I kicked these guides to the curb, which led to some hard lessons.

In my journey through life, my family has sustained me. They are the precious people who give me strength and support. When the chips are down, I know I can count on them. They have brought me help, hope, comfort, and humor in the hardest of times. They are the ones who joyfully celebrate my achievements and success and cheer me on to new adventures sharing the passions of art, dance, travel, and storytelling.

At this point in my life, I am grateful to be *abuelita*, Nana, and Grandma Susie to my five grandchildren. My desire is to be generous with my time and to share with them the magic of storytelling. They will hear the true story of their great-great-great grandfather, the wagon master. I will share with them the journey of their ancestors from faraway lands and perhaps one of them will become the keeper of our family stories. We dance and paint together, expressing our creativity and imagination, and in the great circle of life I have now become like my Nana. What adventures will they experience? What will be the passions they pursue? How will they affect their communities and the world they will live in? I receive the greatest joy in being a part of the discovery and development of their very own unique paths of True North.

A native of Los Angeles, Susie Brown has lived throughout the state of California as well as Hawaii and Washington. A retired Registered Nurse, Susie has had many other jobs: cook, waitress, directory assistance telephone operator, and special education teacher's assistant. She was a demonstrator of barbeques and household appliances and, until recently, enjoyed sharing culinary tips and treats at her friendly local market.

Her love of reading began at a young age with weekly trips to the library and a set of *My Bookhouse* story books filled with beautiful illustrations that sparked her imagination. As an adult her favorite storytellers include authors Isabel Allende, Barbara Kingsolver, and David Sedaris.

Susie is grateful to be a survivor of cancer and is the mother of three children and grandmother to five. For the past twenty-one years Susie has lived in Laguna Woods Village where some of her Baby Boomer neighbors like to call themselves "Village People." Susie feels this is a true reflection of the sense of community she has experienced. Laguna Woods has over 250 clubs representing a myriad of interests and activities, and Susie has had the opportunity to pursue her love of art with classes in watercolor, ceramics, jewelry, quilting, and film.

In 2008, Susie formed a Gal Pal Club with her neighbors who have become friends and extended family. It has been especially important to have these bonds of friendship and support to stay connected during the 2020 pandemic.

While working with the Rhythm of Life Drum Circle Club Susie shared her collection of percussion instruments from around the world, some gathered in her travels to twenty-two countries. Her passion for travel will be the subject of her future book, and she is also working on a children's book in collaboration with her grandson who is a talented cartoonist.

My Life's Lessons

Joan McConville

I have found my True North—that's the place I know I belong because I have found contentment. My journey took seven decades. Now, it is time to pass on my life lessons to my grandsons, Andrew and Zach. After all, aren't these lessons meant to be shared?

I have two sisters, eight and twelve years older than I. When our parents brought me home from the hospital it was the day before Easter. My sister said, "That's our little Easter Bunny." I was Bunny for the next fifty years. My real name is Bernice—doesn't that sound stuffy? Well, I am not, so Bunny fit me perfectly.

When I was eighteen months old, my parents bought lakefront property in Northern California. This move changed our family dynamic because they became obsessed with creating their dream. When completed, they owned a home, shoe store, shoe repair shop, and three rental cabins, all built by my father. Dad and Mom worked every day. Dad worked in construction during the day and repaired shoes in the evening. My mother managed the shoe store six days a week, cleaned the cabins, and washed the linens and towels with a wringer washing machine. My sisters took care of me and helped with the chores.

My oldest sister married and moved away when I was in the first grade. I didn't know until after she left that she had been protecting me from my parents' fighting. That year I missed 108 days of school. I had stomachaches every day from the stress I was feeling. I was afraid of my dad and afraid of my teacher.

Fortunately, my friends at school were talking about going to Sunday School. I asked my parents if I could go, too. My parents didn't attend church, but they said I could—and that changed my path. Rev. Freeman was a soft-spoken, caring man. He lived in the tiny house next to the church with his beautiful wife. She had long blonde hair that she braided and wrapped around her head like a halo. They had three darling little girls. I remember him telling me how much God loves me. I have since wondered if he knew how troubled I was.

When I was nine, my parents gave me a Bible for Christmas. My name was engraved on the cover in gold letters. My mother was raised in church and knew this was something I would cherish. I had just learned to write in cursive and there was a section for notes. I started looking up all the Bible stories I had heard at church: the 23rd Psalm, the Ten Commandments, the Sermon on the Mount, and the birth of Jesus. As I found each one, I wrote down the page number for that story on my page of notes. The best part was I felt like I was finally a part of God's family. You might say that was my rite of passage. From that point on, I felt as though God was really looking after me. Now, when something unexpected happens, I consider that a wink from God. It's His way of letting me know He is there.

As the years passed, Rev. Freeman was transferred to another church in another town. He had grown our congregation and was needed elsewhere. Rev. Brown took his place. He was a harsh, pulpit-pounding preacher. He kept telling us we were all sinners and were all going to Hell, a far cry from the kind man who told me God loved me and I could talk to him every day. So, I started church hopping. In our small town, there were four main churches. Each had its own flavor, but I didn't hear *God loves me* anymore. Something was missing.

My Life Lesson:
Having faith in God is crucial in difficult times. Prayers
don't have to be lavish. Just talk to God.
He listens. And you will feel better.

Summers growing up on the lake were fun. The families who came for one- or two-week vacations were the happiest. They looked forward to leaving their work and all the chores at home to spend leisure time together. There was boating, swimming, miniature golf, movies, barbeques, and just relaxing. The funny part is, I don't remember learning how to swim, I just always knew I could.

I was ten years old when my family took our only vacation. All I knew was that we were going to Disneyland! It was 1955, the year Disneyland opened; this would be the most magical time of my life. I remember my sister and I looking out the windows of the car when we drove down on the freeway. We were both looking to see who would see the first movie star. No, we didn't see any, but it was fun looking for them.

I didn't anticipate Dad's cruel teasing. When we drove the cars at Autopia and got a driver's license, Dad said, "They shouldn't have given you a license because you're a lousy driver." The next day we went to Point Loma Lighthouse. When we reached the highest point at the lighthouse, I was dizzy. I remember feeling frozen in place; I couldn't take a step because I was so afraid. Again, Dad said, "Look how scared she is. She can't even move!" He was laughing, but I wasn't.

Next, we went on an excursion on San Diego Bay. I took pictures all day with my new camera. As we left the ship we saw a sign that said *No Photography Allowed.* Dad said, "You're going to be arrested for taking pictures of our naval fleet." I was afraid my film would be taken away and it wasn't even developed yet.

After that we visited the San Diego Zoo. I had a donut left from breakfast and threw it to the bear. Trying to get to the donut, the bear fell into the dry moat, and the trainer had to come and get him out.

This wasn't the vacation I saw other families enjoying. Were my expectations too high? In my mind, selling the resort, shoe store, and shoe repair business would make everything better, but I was wrong. Dad became obsessed with building our new house and the fighting continued.

My Life Lesson:
Always take a vacation. Let the whole family make plans
together. Half the fun is the anticipation of the adventure.
Families make the best memories together.

In high school, I became an over-achiever. I was class president, cheerleader, yearbook editor, and in every after-school program—so I wouldn't have to go home. In my junior year, I dated a guy who was a year older than me. For the first time I felt loved. On Sunday nights, I went to his house. His mother made homemade hamburgers and French fries for dinner and we sat in the living room with TV trays watching *The Wonderful World of Disney*. His family was kind and there were lots of laughs. This is what I felt family should be like.

By the end of my first year in college, I was pregnant and married my high school sweetheart. This wasn't what we had planned, but we were in love and I knew we would live happily ever after. The first summer we both worked at the lake—this was a resort town and work was seasonal. When summer was over we moved to Santa Rosa where my husband worked as a forklift driver during the day and attended college at night.

A few weeks before Jane was born, I was really touched by a story in a magazine about babies who were switched at birth. The babies were about five years old when the article was written and one of them was ill. When the doctors looked for a donor, they realized neither parent was a match. Checking the hospital records, they found another baby who was born at the same time was a match. The dilemma was should they return the girls to their natural parents or leave them in the homes where they had been growing up? I told my husband we must be very careful that we get our baby. He tried to console me by saying that was years ago and there are precautions to prevent that from happening. The day after our beautiful baby girl was born, I was allowed to walk to the nursery to view the babies. There were eleven babies in the nursery—our girl and ten boys! What are the odds of that ever happening? Do you think God knew how much I was worried about this and gave me a wink?

My Life Lesson:
Marry your true love. The best relationships are built on friendship and trust. When you find that person, treasure every day together.

Three years later, we were blessed with a second baby girl, Susie. That same year we bought our first house. Three years after that, we welcomed our third baby girl, Karen. Life was good. I was able to stay at home with the girls while my husband worked as an accountant.

When it was time to replace our Chevelle station wagon, we went to the dealership looking for a family car. This was the era before soccer mom cars. We looked at station wagons and then we saw a Dodge van with a camper conversion. I thought that would be ideal for our family because I desperately wanted us to go on vacations like the families I knew while growing up. We didn't think we could afford it. The salesman approached us and explained the monthly payments would be the same as the station wagon; however, we would make payments for five years instead of three years. Why not?

That was one of the best decisions we ever made. We enjoyed many weekend trips and vacations in our van. At that time, we didn't need a reservation at a campground. On Fridays I bought groceries and packed the van. After dinner, we climbed in and went off on an adventure. The girls usually fell asleep during the drive, so when they woke up in the morning, they explored the beach, the lake, or the campground.

I remember one trip to Manchester State Beach with two other families. We played at the beach that day and when we were walking back to the campground Jane said she knew the way and asked if she could run ahead of us. She was off in a flash, only to return minutes later with a frightened look on her face. When we asked what was wrong, she told us she had seen a skunk and it ran into the women's restroom. I couldn't imagine a skunk at the ocean; don't they live in the forest? We didn't use that restroom the rest of the weekend, just in case he was still there. Years later, I saw a skunk at the ocean and knew Jane had been right.

When we had outgrown our first house, my husband was on caravan with his real estate office and found a bigger house for us. It was the house families dream of—four bedrooms and two bathrooms upstairs and a big living room, family room, dining room, bathroom, and kitchen downstairs. It was located at the end of a cul-de-sac with an eight-acre park next door and an elementary school on the other side of the park. We put a deposit on it that day. When Jane and Susie came home from school, Karen told them, "We bought a new house today. I got to see it and you didn't!" Susie was fine with that. But Jane, who was in middle school, couldn't believe we would do such a thing without her knowledge. Needless to say, it was the perfect house in the perfect location for us. A God wink for sure!

My Life Lesson:
Cherish the life-changing moments. A new baby, a new
car, a new house; these are milestones that highlight our
achievements and give us encouragement.

Being a mom was what I always wanted to be. That was my most treasured role. But I want to share the lessons I learned in the working world with Andrew and Zach as they begin their careers. They can learn from the challenges I faced and other lessons about people, wisdom, and integrity.

After being a stay-at-home mom for fourteen years I found a part-time position in a dental office scheduling appointments and making collection calls. The transition was easier than I expected. A few months later, the dental assistant didn't show up for work, so the dentist asked me to help with the patients. He assured me he would tell me what to do and I would be fine. I was worried about the lady who didn't come to work, so I called her to see if she was okay. She told me he had fired her. I was too naïve to know this was a big red flag.

The dentist registered me for classes so I could learn to take dental X-rays. Then, I took night classes at the local college to obtain my license as a Registered Dental Assistant. I felt I was on a good career path that would benefit my family. The state licensing exam was in Sacramento, so our whole family went, including the exchange student from Japan who was staying with us at the time. While I took the exam, my family went to the zoo and the park. It was a stressful day for me, but afterwards I joined my family for fun at the park. It was always good to be with my family, no matter how tough the day was.

One year later, the dentist moved his practice to a new location, paying four times the rent he had paid in the past. In no time, he called to tell me that his wife was taking my position. He came to my house that evening to pick up my office keys. What a shock! Sometimes I miss the red flags. Sometimes I don't want to see them.

I started a new job assisting another dentist. This one had a very short temper. He threw towels, raised his voice, and had little regard for the people who worked for him. I had put up with this behavior from my dad for years but would not allow my boss to do this. At the end of the first week, I gave my two-week notice. Was I learning to see the red flags?

My Life Lesson:
Never be afraid to stand up for yourself!
The truth is, if you don't stand for something,
you will fall for anything.
Value yourself so others will value you.

That same week, my husband took Susie to see the eye doctor. He knew the bookkeeper and she asked about our family. He told her I was looking for a job and learned that they needed a receptionist. A few days later, I interviewed with the doctor during my lunch hour and started my new position the Monday following my last day with the dentist. Another God wink.

A few months later, the ophthalmic assistant went on maternity leave. The doctor asked me to help him with patients. Seems familiar, doesn't it? The doctor had just hired an optometrist fresh out of college who was eager to teach me everything he knew. By the time the other assistant returned from maternity leave, she was assigned to a newly hired ophthalmologist and I remained with the original doctor. She felt I had taken her job. There was some tension in the office, but it wasn't my choice.

A couple of years later, I was offered a part-time position in registration at the local hospital. This was an opportunity to learn a computer system and have more time at home. My status was part time, meaning no benefits, but that didn't matter because our family was insured through my husband's company. I learned the computer system quickly and was able to work in registration in the Admissions, Emergency Room, and Same Day Care departments. This meant that I could pick up extra hours when someone called in sick or went on vacation but I could choose if I wanted extra shifts or not. Most of the time, I worked five or six shifts a week. One day, I went to my supervisor to request full-time status with benefits, including vacation time and sick days, since I was working full time. She told me that there wasn't a full-time position open in that department. I applied for full-time openings in other departments but was never interviewed for any of those positions. I was asked to do bed coordination Monday through Friday from 8 a.m. to 5 p.m. That was full time, but my status was still part time because I was working in the same department. Previously, bed assignments were made by the charge nurse. It was more cost effective for me to perform that task.

An oncologist I knew came into the hospital and asked me to work for him. He said he would pay me at a higher rate and I would only work thirty-six hours a week and would have Thursday afternoons and every weekend off. That sounded wonderful! I accepted the position and turned in my resignation. On my last day at the hospital, the Director of Human Resources invited me to his office for an exit interview. While we talked, I asked him if I could see my employment file. He thought that was an unusual request but handed the file to me. I looked at the file and handed it back to him. He asked, "What were you looking for?" I replied, "I applied for four full-time positions over the last few years, but none of my applications are in my file." It was clear to me that someone had intercepted my applications, which is why I was never interviewed.

My Life Lesson:
Life isn't fair. Let go and move on.
Holding on to a hurt or rejection keeps you from
moving forward with a positive attitude.

I managed the oncology practice for the next three years, until the doctor moved his practice out of state. About that time, my husband was passed up for a promotion, so we sold our home and moved to the central coast of California. I looked at this as an adventure—a new place and a new beginning.

I wanted to start my own business. Jane had been working in recycling for the city of Pasadena and she sent me several brochures about selling recycled stationery products. I was pretty excited about the prospect and wanted to rent store space and teach elementary students how to recycle and make recycled paper. My husband was not supportive of that idea, so I went to work as a temp at an escrow company. I did that for a few months, but when the temporary position ended, I went to work as an independent interior designer. A year later, I discovered the reason I wasn't making sales was because the lady I worked with had a reputation for over-charging and under-delivering, and no one trusted this organization.

I discovered a family-owned furniture manufacturing company in the next city. Thinking I had just received a God wink, I jumped in with both feet. I went on appointments and helped clients choose fabrics and colors for their rooms, but the commissions were few and far between. My boss told me he wanted to step up his advertising and asked me to enter the reverse telephone directory into his computer so he could create a mailing list of every resident in the county. I would be paid hourly for the data entry, so that sounded great. I could learn another computer system and actually be paid for the work. Once I got into the computer system, I stumbled onto the invoices: all the clients I had seen during the week came back on the weekend and my boss's father wrote up their orders, made the sale, and received the commissions for the work I had done. Feeling defeated once again, I went to the employment agency seeking a new job.

My Life Lesson:
Be careful who you trust. Recognize the red flags!
A person with integrity acts the same
regardless of who is in the room.

Thankfully, I was hired immediately by the local ophthalmology group, which had four offices and three physicians. You guessed it! I was working in the back office and I was back in class. This time, I was taking a home study course to be a Certified Ophthalmic Assistant. A few months later, I was promoted to Medical Staff Supervisor. When they opened another office, I was asked to interview candidates for an assistant for the new doctor. I asked him what skills were important to him. He said, "Hire someone nice. I can teach the skills

I need. I can't teach someone to be nice." I will never forget that. He was right!

Things were going well. One morning I was scheduled to work at one of the satellite offices. The Office Manager from the main office asked me to deliver the paycheck to the receptionist at that office. When I got out of my car, the check fell on the ground. I picked it up and saw that her pay was much higher than mine. How could this be? She greeted patients half a day and sent the billing to the main office. Words cannot describe how much this upset me. I continued to work for the next few weeks not knowing what to do. I couldn't tell my boss I had seen the receptionist's paycheck.

My Life Lesson:
Live with your own conscience.
Take time to figure things out. We are never
persuasive when we are abrasive.

At home we were struggling financially. My husband was selling real estate and the market was at an all-time low. I took a two-week vacation and went to visit my daughter and son-in-law. Jane was very close to delivering my first grandson, Andrew. This was an exciting time for her and I wanted to be with her. When I told her my story she said, "Mom, you could make a lot more money down here." She helped me write a new resume and I scheduled a few interviews for the following week.

The birth of my first grandson was the distraction I needed. I felt so much joy seeing this little baby and holding him. I didn't want to go back home. When I did, my heart was not in my work. A few weeks later I received calls from two offices where I had sent my resume and they wanted to interview me. This was a chance to see my grandson again. I was happy to make the trip.

The first interview went well, but I was not impressed with the office staff. This wasn't a working team. I could recognize the red flags! The second interview was later that day. When I arrived, I introduced myself and said I had an appointment with the manager. The receptionist told me I was mistaken; he was out of town. How could that be? I drove all that way!

Discouraged, I drove home and went back to work. Two weeks later, I received a call from that manager. He said, "I am so sorry I missed you the day you came for your interview. I know you are the perfect fit for this position. Please come back for an interview and I will make time for you, even on a weekend." It just so happened that my husband and I were going to visit our daughter and her family the following weekend and attend his cousin's wedding reception. I met the manager that Sunday morning and after a two-hour interview and a tour of the office, he offered me the position. The salary was significantly more than I was making.

On the way home, my husband said I should take the job. He would sell our house and he would join me. I gave my notice and moved a few weeks later. The first week I stayed with Jane and her family. The next week Karen, my youngest daughter, and I rented a house nearby. Karen became Andrew's nanny. I felt like everything was falling into place and this was where I was supposed to be. Was this my True North?

When I made this move, I thought about the times that I had been overlooked in the workforce. I had that aha moment when I thought, "No one can take Bunny seriously, but I hate Bernice. I will start using my middle name, Joan." The transition was seamless. I moved to a new location, started a new job, and used a new first name. Things would be better now!

My new job was so much easier. Instead of three doctors in five locations, I was supervising the staff of two doctors in one office. I adjusted to my new life. My husband had no intention of joining me and said, "I don't want to live in Southern California." Two years later, I filed for divorce.

My Life Lesson:
Life has many seasons. Live in the season you are in.
Always cherish the memories from the other seasons.

Feeling restless and a little lost, I began taking classes at a local college on the weekend, pursuing my dream of writing children's books. I took a day off to study for exams. When I returned to my office there was a letter on my desk notifying me that the office was closing in three weeks and my severance pay would be one week for each year served. I wasn't surprised. The two doctors had opened a second office and hired a third doctor. There had been so much friction between them I knew the end was near. I was a little older and a little wiser.

I landed a position in an escrow company and went back to escrow classes at night; my writing would have to wait. After a few months I knew this office was not a good match for me. Jane and her family had moved back to Napa and she suggested I join them. What a great idea! By then I had two grandsons and I could watch them grow up.

I started with a temp position that evolved into a permanent position with a renowned Napa Valley winery. All was well for a time. When the Board of Directors talked of selling the winery, I knew I would be out of work again, so I proactively moved to Southern California where jobs were plentiful. I was back in escrow, but with the market decline three years later, I was out of a job again. For the next seven years I worked in the insurance industry.

When I moved to Southern California I wanted to find a neighborhood church. The man who is now my son-in-law invited me to his church. I quickly realized I was depending on my own strength, not developing my relationship with God. I learned the value of true friendships and how important it is to be part of a community of believers.

I was able to take some wonderful vacations with my daughters and grandsons. We went to Alaska for a week, then on three cruises to the Caribbean islands. My greatest joy was spending time with them and sharing our adventures together. Vacations and family go together. They were so important to me. The laughter we shared and the countless games of Bananagrams are priceless.

My Life Lesson:
A career is how you make your living.
Living is loving your life. Don't let making a living
get in the way of living.

At age sixty-nine, I quit that job and was fortunate to find my True North. My definition of True North is being in a place of complete peace. I am currently working part time at a regional campus of my church. I work with an amazing staff of caring adults who minister to seniors. What a joy! The journey was worth every setback and every experience.

Andrew has graduated from CSU San Diego. He is a wonderful, caring man with a big heart and an entrepreneurial spirit. Zach will soon graduate from CSU Long Beach. He has many talents and will find his True North if he follows his heart.

My message to both of them is this: the past is where you learn the lessons; the future is where you apply the lessons. Use my lessons to guide you along the way. Life is a journey. Enjoy every moment! I love both of you unconditionally and forever!

It has taken Joan McConville seven decades to find her "True North." She works part time for her local church providing services to seniors in assisted living communities. Joan has learned that life is a journey. She embraces the challenges and allows the journey to transform into an adventure.

Joan has had a passion for books ever since she learned to read. She grew up in a small town without a library where the monthly bookmobile visits were always a welcome treat.

As her children were growing up, Joan developed a passion specifically for children's books. Her dream was to write colorful stories with an intentional message of being good, doing good, and caring for others—with whimsy and humor, of course. The real drawback was her lack of artistic talent. Children's books require wonderful pictures to bring them to life.

Then along came videos. She went back to college to take media classes and imagined producing her stories on video. The following year, she relocated for a career change and the dream of writing vanished only to surface again years later.

Recently, she talked to friends about leaving a legacy. Really? Write her life story? Why not?! This anthology project gave her the opportunity to share some of her stories about life and the lessons she learned with her two grandsons. It became a labor of love. Was this her True North? Joan says her True North is being where she is happy and content. She knows she has arrived because there's no place she'd rather be.

This is the second anthology for Joan. The first one was *The Pivot Project*, published in 2020. If you enjoy reading Joan's chapters in either book, please let her know. She would appreciate your comments, good or bad. After all, isn't that how we grow?

You can email Joan at joanmcconville@att.net. She might even invite you for tea and homemade cookies.

Acknowledgments

First and foremost, I am deeply grateful that I have been Divinely guided to help writers become authors and share my talents with others. I am thankful for all the amazing people in my life, including my clients, friends, and family.

Thank you to my family, Mom, Dad, Jane, Andrew, Zach, Karen, and Mat, for their love and support as I firmly set my sights on becoming a guide for authors to find their voice and their True North. Special thanks to my mom, Joan (Bunny) McConville, for bringing me into this world and always giving love freely...not just to me, but to everyone in her life. You make me a better person with your daily demonstration of faith, love, and compassion.

Thank you to Stacy and Farrell Rodrigues, and Peggy Graham, for being my second family. Stacy, our conversations and ruminations over the last year have been a very important part of me finding my own voice. Thank you for being you.

To the team that helped *A Path to Purpose: Seven Inspired Stories to Discover Your True North* come to life—Bonnie McDermid, Amy Scott, and Michelle White—thank you for your expertise and being a part of something awesome. Each of you have a special place in my heart.

To the contributing authors of *A Path to Purpose*: Thank you Debra, Esthela, Joan, Kirby, Georgia, Shara, and Susie B. Each of you has been a joy to work with and share this experience with, and I am blessed by your friendship. You are the reason this book has been created. I am deeply humbled that you have trusted me to share your stories with the world and I am grateful to have walked the path with you.

As all of these stories demonstrate, we take what we learn as children to live our lives in hopes that we find our True North. The work that is done to inspire children to live spiritual lives is evident through the mission of the Center for Spiritual Living in Fort Lauderdale, Florida. A portion of the proceeds of book sales from *A Path to Purpose* will be donated to the Center for Spiritual Living to help raise awareness that the children of today are truly our future.

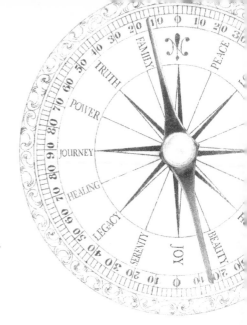

About the Author

Susie Schaefer believes that books are the gateway to creating a movement. Her love of books goes far beyond the feel of a fabric cover or the smell of a library. Susie honors and empowers storytellers to be part of the global conversation and create a ripple effect through books. Working with business owners brings her tremendous joy, particularly when an author's book tells their own personal story and creates "Business Ascension" by melding an author's mission and message.

Susie hails from corporate America teaching and training, becoming a marketing expert, working with non-profits, and in radio broadcasting and commercial acting. Susie has been called "the Book Angel" by her clients and skillfully guides authors through the independent publishing process to finish that dream book, launch a speaking career, or build a business with a book that gets results and gives back.

Susie's understanding of social impact or "cause" publishing enables her to offer a unique foundation for publishing by building community, creating connections, and being the catalyst for change. When not reading or publishing books, Susie can be found practicing her downward dog (yoga), meditating on the beach, or planning her next travel adventure.

- **Behind the Scenes,** a six-month interactive program that takes a group of authors through writing, editing, design, publishing, and book marketing. Each contributing author writes a single chapter to produce a themed anthology.
- **Author Evolution:** Four Months to Create a Book that Gets Results and Gives Back, a self-paced online program to help authors learn how to independently publish...from start to finish.
- **The Amazon Best Seller Campaign,** a service for published authors to get their books positioned for Best Seller status and future book marketing.
- **Private Client Publishing Services** to help you create your desired book and successfully publish independently, while keeping 100% of your rights and royalties.

A complimentary 30-minute consultation
is available to discover your next steps
to becoming an independently published author.

To connect, visit www.FinishTheBookPublishing.com.